Teaching Minds

How Cognitive Science Can Save Our Schools

Teaching Minds

How Cognitive Science Can Save Our Schools

ROGER SCHANK

Teachers College, Columbia University
New York and London

Published by Teachers College Press, 1234 Amsterdam Avenue, New York, NY 10027

Library of Congress Cataloging-in-Publication Data

Schank, Roger C., 1946—
Teaching minds : how cognitive science can save our schools / Roger Schank.
   p. cm.
  Includes bibliographical references.
  ISBN 978-0-8077-5266-1 (pbk. : alk. paper) — ISBN 978-0-8077-5267-8 (hardcover : alk. paper)
  1. Cognitive learning. 2. Learning, Psychology of. 3. Cognitive science. 4. Education. I. Title.
  LB1060.S34 2011
  370.15'23--dc23

                        2011025569

ISBN 978-0-8077-5266-1 (paper)
ISBN 978-0-8077-5267-8 (hardcover)

Printed on acid-free paper
Manufactured in the United States of America

18 17 16 15 14 13 12 11   8 7 6 5 4 3 2 1

For Milo (who can now read this) and for Max, Mira, and Jonah

Contents

Preface   ix

1. Cognitive Process-Based Education   1

2. Teaching Kids to Walk and Talk   15

3. What Can't You Teach?   35

4. Twelve Cognitive Processes
   That Underlie Learning   45

5. Real-Life Learning Projects Considered   57

6. A Socratic Dialogue   73

7. Knowledge-Based Education vs.
   Process-Based Education   75

8. New Curricula for a New Way of Teaching   89

9. How to Teach the Twelve Cognitive
   Processes That Underlie Learning   109

10. Defining Intelligence   137

11. Restructuring the University   157

12. How Not to Teach   171

13. How the Best Universities
    Inadvertently Ruin Our Schools   183

14. What Can We Do About It?   205

Notes   221

About the Author   223

Preface

My father always told me that I would be a teacher. He didn't mean it in a nice way. My father talked in riddles. As the only child in the house, I had plenty of time and opportunity to figure out what he was really saying. This was it: I am afraid that like me, the best you will be able to do in life is to be a civil service worker. He was also saying: If he had realized he was going to be a civil service worker, at least he could have been a teacher, which he might have enjoyed. He wasn't really talking about me at all.

I never had any intention of being a teacher. I didn't particularly like school and later, when I became a professor, the part of the job I disliked the most was the teaching. One might wonder how I wound up being a professor if I disliked teaching, and one might wonder why I am writing a book about teaching if I dislike teaching. One also might wonder whether I still dislike teaching. Yes. And no. It depends on what one means by teaching, which is, after all, what this book is about.

The other day my 3-year-old grandson Milo told me he was going to teach me how to throw rocks. It seemed an odd idea. What could he mean by this? To Milo, "teach" means to tell someone what to do and how to do it and then have the person do it too. Teach is part of tell plus imitate for Milo. Milo is 3. It is not too surprising that this is what teach means to him. It is a little surprising that he thinks he should be his grandfather's teacher, but that is another issue. But it is really no shock that Milo thinks this is what teach means. It is what nearly everyone thinks teach means. The commonly accepted usage of teach is tell and then have the person who was told, do what he was told. This certainly is not what teach ought to mean, or more important, is not what good teaching is. And, every good teacher knows this. The problem is that the system that employs teachers doesn't know it and more or less insists that Milo's definition be the one that is followed.

Actually, I am being too generous here. Milo's view, namely, that after he tells me, I will do what he has said, is a better definition of teaching than the one actually employed commonly today. Milo at least thinks that the end result will be the student doing something that the teacher did. In school, teach usually means helping the student to know something that the teacher told him. Milo doesn't know about that definition of teaching yet since he hasn't been to school, but, unfortunately, he soon will.

I have been thinking about teaching for more than 50 years. First I thought about it when my father said that was what I was going to be. Then I thought about it as I watched my teachers teach me and, no less important, watched my father teach me.

My father eventually retired from his civil service job and became a junior high school teacher in Harlem. He loved his new job and, I have to assume, became a good teacher. I say it that way because he was certainly not a good teacher for me, at least not when he thought he was trying to teach me. I remember him trying to teach me algebra and it making no sense to me whatever. I remember him teaching me sports and I mostly think of him as being totally frustrated with my inability to perform as well as he had hoped. (Being a jock was a big thing to my father.)

I did fine in algebra without his help and, in fact, became a math major in college. But, as I look back at it, my father was my first and best teacher. Why do I say this after all the bad things I have just said? Because my father was at his best when he wasn't teaching but was just saying what was on his mind and arguing. He often talked about history because he liked history. And when he talked about history and I asked questions, he became a good Socratic teacher. He forced me to think and question in our discussions. The conversations were often very heated but also were a highlight of my intellectual life at that time. My father didn't teach me anything except how to think. That's better than algebra, actually. For this I am grateful.

So, I thought about teaching then and I thought about it again when I went to college. As part of my father's conversations with me about life, he talked a great deal about his own experiences. His mother sent him to New York City to live with his aunt in Brooklyn and to go to college. He was 15 and had, until that time, spent his entire life on a farm/hotel run by his parents in upstate New York. He was unprepared for the city, had no money, missed his family, and had no idea why he wanted to go to college at all. Did I mention that he was 15? He had graduated first in his class (a class of 16, I think) and had skipped a few grades on the way. Suddenly he found himself at New York University, which in those days was located in the Bronx.

This is what he remembered most about college in 1923: Apart from the poverty stories, the "how hard he had to work to support himself" stories, the stories about watching the Yankees from the elevated train and wishing he could go to a game, he remembered that teachers lectured, that you had to memorize what they told you and then tell it back to them on a test. He thought college was stupid, but he assured me (in 1960) that college surely had changed by now and that teachers wouldn't still be doing this. Oh yeah? In 1962, when I entered college, they were doing exactly that. And, in 2000, when I retired from 32 years of professoring, not that much had changed.

So I was thinking about teaching before I got to college and I was thinking about it while I was a professor and I am thinking about it now that I have, for the most part, finished teaching. To make sure I have been thinking about it correctly, I asked former Ph.D. students of mine, (now tenured professors mostly and some industry executives) what they had learned from me while they were spending 4–7 years studying with me. I thought their answers might help me think about teaching in a new way. I sent an e-mail to maybe 20 former students whose e-mail addresses I happened to have, and most responded. Here are some excerpts.

1. I remember quite specifically a homework presentation I made in your class. When I presented it in class, I was a junior in college, and all the other students in that class were grad students. When I was done you smiled at everyone (a rare event) and said, "Anyone care to follow that act?" Your clearly heartfelt endorsement of my little research product was a key moment in my coming to trust my own ideas. I just submitted a $16.7 million proposal to NIH that would create the first all-computational genome center. The kind of chutzpah embodied in that proposal is one consequence of my experience with you.

2. The way you assigned me to a project—you sent me to each existing project for 2 weeks until I hit on a project with a good fit (I was enthusiastic and coherent talking about it). I used this technique when I was assigning people at Accenture.

3. You taught me to teach by telling students stories that are meaningful to you. I think to be a real teacher you have to let yourself be vulnerable. So the students can see that you are a human with feelings and fears and goals. And then being able to say to the students: This is the way I do it; it fits who I am; it helps me be successful; and don't let anyone tell you that you can't do something.

4. You taught me that not everyone will like you no matter what you do and no matter how hard you try. I came back from a Deloitte course evaluation, and the deans just hated me. Instead of being upset with me, you assured me that you have to just say what you believe, and some people won't like you, and oh well.

5. You taught me to start by collecting data. I recall watching most of your papers start by collection of data. I recall watching your criticisms of work that was just abstraction on abstraction, with no data at its roots.

6. You once told me to imagine that my mother was my audience—if I could explain it to my mother, I could explain it to anyone. Incredibly, this seems to work for every audience out there. So I've passed that tip along to my students and it seems to work for them too.

7. I remember that you used to tell us we need to be excited to get up and go to work in the morning, that that was the most important thing. For some people, it's because of the people you will be with. For some, it is because of the passion about whatever it is. But, in general, I still give people that advice (and it is advice I've also been giving my own kids). You have to love what you are doing.

This is just a sample but it reflects what these former students, now all in their 40s and 50s, remember about what I taught them. Hadn't they learned any facts from me? Didn't I teach them some real stuff? Some said in passing that they had learned the actual content of the subjects I taught as well, but that that wasn't as important to them as the things they chose to write about. Why not?

There are two important answers to this question and those answers are what this book is really about. My father offered these same answers to me, not explicitly by any means, when I thought about the good and bad of having him as my teacher. When he tried to teach me facts, I learned nothing much. When he engaged my mind, I learned a lot. As a professor I never forgot this lesson. I rarely tried to teach facts, upsetting many a student along the way. I just argued with them, or encouraged them. I never told them much, except maybe some good stories.

So here are the answers:

The first is:

Teaching isn't what outsiders to the profession think it is.

The profession I am referring to here is, of course, the teaching profession.

The second is:

Learning isn't what outsiders to the profession think it is.

In this case, the profession I am referring to is not teaching at all.

Let's start with teaching.

A professor friend of mine once asked her class what they thought a professor's biggest fear was while teaching a class. They all agreed it was not knowing the answer to a question a student might ask. When she told this story to a group of professors, they all laughed out loud.

Why am I telling this story? Because a student's view of teaching varies greatly from a teacher's view. No teacher worries about not knowing the right answer to something a student will ask. You can always fake it (say—*What do you think?* or, *Class, can you help here?*) if you think it is important, but answers don't matter very much. Teachers are not supposed to be encyclopedias. They are supposed to be something else. The question is: *What?*

My students' responses above give a hint. Teachers are supposed to be people who help students find their interests in life, think about how to make decisions, understand how to approach a problem, or otherwise live sensibly. Teachers are never shocked to be asked to provide personal or professional advice to a student having a problem—any problem. If one takes one's job seriously, teaching means being available to help. But this important advisory job is confused by lesson plans, and class hours, and lectures, none of which matter very much.

Why do I say that these things don't matter very much? This is the essence of what this book is about—the move from content-based instruction to cognitive-based learning, assisted by good teaching. This means we will have to define this "new" kind of learning (it's not really new, of course, just new to schools) and the "new" kind of teaching that is a natural consequence of using this new learning method.

Most teachers understand and appreciate that delivering the required material is not their real job, at least it is not the reason they signed on in the first place. The employers of teachers, on the other hand—administrators, governments, department heads, and so on—expect certain material to be covered. Exciting students is not on their worry list. This is a big problem for teachers and for students, and one that we will address here.

But my more serious concern is our conception of learning, not teaching. Teaching follows one's conception of learning so getting learning right is of prime importance. When I said earlier that outsiders to the learning profession wouldn't get the real point, I was being ironic. There is no learning profession. Why not?

In 1989, I moved from Yale to Northwestern to establish a new institute, funded by Andersen Consulting, devoted to issues of changing training and education by the use of new technologies. I needed a name for the institute and came up with The Institute for the Learning Sciences. I made up the term *learning sciences*. There was no such field in academia. Most people thought I meant we were planning to work on how people learned science. The only academic fields that "studied" learning were psychology and education. Psychology, being an experimental field, allows faculty to work only on experiments about learning that provide data in a controlled environment. Education faculty study how schools work and very rarely think about learning outside of the school context or in a way different from the paradigm already extant in schools. I wanted to create a learning profession. In 1989, there certainly didn't seem to be one.

Today this is less true. Cognitive science, a field I also had a big part in creating, has become more important in the academic world. Training, and e-learning, the first new field to come about as a result of our work at my new institute (for better or for worse, I am not too fond of most e-learning work) have become more important to think about within the academic context, in part because online courses are seen as potential revenue producers.

So, while there is still no learning profession per se, there is much interest in what learning is about. This book is meant to address the issue of what learning really is, in or out of school, and to answer the question: How does learning really work? The questions that follow from the answer to that question are:

- What kinds of learning situations occur naturally?
- How can we focus education (and training and e-learning) on those types of situations in a new paradigm?
- What would teaching look like in this new paradigm?
- If what we know about how learning works is antithetical to how school works, then what can we do?

Answering these questions is one goal of this book.

Another goal of this book is to think seriously about what it means to teach. Typically, we look at teaching in precisely the way that our system forces us to look at it. There are subjects and there are experts, and experts talk about their subjects to students who listen to what they have to say. This idea is not only archaic—it is wrong. In the history of humankind, teaching could never have looked this way.

Until recently, teaching always meant apprenticeship. We are set up to be apprentices, to learn by doing with help from a mentor. We have done this since the beginning of time. When learning became academic in nature, when students were expected to become scholars, all this changed—and it didn't change for the better. Teaching started to mean talking, and talking is a terrible way to teach. People aren't really that good at listening, after all. Small children don't listen to their parents. They may copy their parents. They can be corrected by their parents. They may be impeded from doing something by their parents. But listen? Not really. We listen in order to be entertained, not in order to learn.

This lack of understanding about what learning really is like, and what teaching must be like in order to be useful, has caused us to set up school in a way that really does not work very well. When students complain about school, when politicians say school isn't working, we understand that there is a problem. But we don't understand what the problem is. We think we can fix schools by making them more friendly, or safer, or paying teachers better, or having students have more say, or obsessing about test scores, but none of this is the case.

The problem with schools lies in our conception of the role of school. We see school as a place to study academics, to become a scholar, when in fact very few students actually want to become scholars or study academics.

As a society we have gotten caught up in a conception of school from the late 1800s that has failed to change in any significant way, despite the fact that universal education has made the system unstable. Universities dominate the discussion, and everyone listens to what academics have to say because they don't see the alternative or know whom else to listen to. But, if we understand how learning actually works, and how teaching actually should work, the alternative becomes much clearer.

It is establishing that clarity that is my goal in this book.

CHAPTER 1

Cognitive Process-Based Education

Education is an admirable thing, but it is well to remember from time to time that nothing that is worth knowing can be taught.

—Oscar Wilde

Learning begins with a goal. However, when we think about education and school, we often forget this. Someone, somewhere, decides that a student must learn about Napoleon, but fails to ask how such learning might conform to a goal that the student consciously holds. We don't forget this when we try to teach a child to walk or talk, because we know that the child does want to learn to do these things. When we teach a child to hit a baseball, we usually determine beforehand that the child wants to learn to do this. But, we forget this simple idea of goal-directed learning as soon as we design curricula for schools. Who cares if the child wants to learn long division? Make the child learn it. It is very important. Full speed ahead!

Somewhere along the way, many students get lost. They may get lost in high school, or in college, or in job training. But somewhere they learn to shut off their natural learning instincts, the ones that drive them to improve because they really want to accomplish something. Instead they try hard to do what they were told to do—they study, they pass tests, and eventually their love of learning is gone. The feedback that they previously have gotten from accomplishing a real goal, one that they truly had held, has been replaced by pleasing the teacher, or getting a good grade, or progress in their goal of getting into a "good college."

Designers (and teachers) of courses must contend with this truth: The students that you have may not want to learn what it is that you want to teach.

What to do?

1

First, we must establish whether students can learn whatever it is that you want to teach. I always wanted to teach my daughter to throw a ball properly. She threw a football astonishingly well at the age of 6. But, she never got it about how to throw a softball. I don't know why. She just couldn't learn to do it right. She can't do math either. Believe me, I tried.

Second, we must determine whether what you want to teach can be taught. Not everything can be taught. It is hard to learn to be a nice guy if you are inclined to be nasty. You can learn to be nicer, or at least to fake it, perhaps, but certain things are hard to learn after a certain age. You can teach a 2-year-old to be nice—a 22-year-old is another story.

Third, we must figure out what method of learning actually would teach what we want to teach. This is an important question that is made more important, in part, by the fact that the learning methods available in schools tend to be of a certain type. The things that schools desire to teach are of a type that conforms to the available methodologies for teaching. Content that lies outside the range of the currently available methodologies typically is not considered something worth teaching.

Fourth, we must decide whether a selected learning methodology actually will work, given the time constraints and abilities of the students, and other constraints that actually exist. This is, of course, the real problem in education. It is easy to say that students would learn better if they had real experiences to draw upon. This isn't that hard to figure out. What is hard is implementing this idea within the time constraints of the school day and the other demands of the school year.

Fifth, we must determine a way that will make what you want to teach fit more closely with real-life goals that your students actually may have. By real-life goals I mean things like walking and talking (and later driving). Why is it that teachers, or more accurately school systems and governments, want to teach things that are not in accord with a student's real interest? While we argue about how best to teach algebra, no one ever asks what to do if a student doesn't want to learn algebra. The question is so weird; the possibility that you could skip algebra because it doesn't interest you is so remote that we don't even think about this in any way. What is the real cause of this problem? Why can't we just let students learn what interests them? Are the people who run schools simply out of touch with how learning really works or how actual students behave when faced with something they

don't want to learn, or is something else more complex going on?
I will summarize these five issues as follows:

ABILITY
POSSIBILITY
METHODOLOGY
CONSTRAINTS
GOAL ALIGNMENT

School is subject-based and, further, those subjects are predefined and agreed upon by those in charge. Without giving a history of how this state of affairs came to be,[1] or why it is an issue, it is first necessary to note that it is the case. I say this because when we were students in school, we accepted the fact that school was the way it was, and we assumed that it was the way it was supposed to be. We may not think each subject we learn is valuable or interesting, and perhaps we long to learn different subjects, but never do we hear people suggest that there shouldn't be subjects in school at all. This is a very difficult idea to swallow. There have always been subjects. What else would there be? What would it mean to not have subjects?

Answering this question is the aim of this book. We need to understand what goes on in schools and what might be preferable. The issue really is not schooling at all. The real issue is how learning actually takes place in the human mind.

Ask a student how he is doing in school and he will tell you the subjects he likes. *I like English but I am bad at math*, he might say. This is such a normal sentiment among students that we never think about how weird a sentiment it really is. We don't ask: *How are you doing at life?* We could ask that of a teenager and she might say: *I am good at dating but bad at driving.*

But, actually, you would never hear teenagers say something like that. This is weird because, in general, dating and driving are much more important subjects in a teenager's world than English and math. But they don't talk about whether they are good at it or bad at it in the same way.

They continue to practice and get better at those things because they care about them. Saying, *I am bad at math,* means, in essence, *. . . and I don't care and have stopped trying because I don't see the point.* Saying, *I am good at English*, typically means, *I am getting a good grade in English.* This state of affairs defines the main problem in education:

There are subjects that are school subjects and there are subjects that are life subjects and teenagers can tell the difference. They work harder at the life subjects.

And, what is the difference between these two kinds of subjects? Goals. It is as simple as that.

Instead of simply saying what is wrong with schools and what teenagers are really like in school, I want to take a different tack.

Some teenagers wake up in the morning wanting to learn history or algebra but they are a very small minority of the school population. There is no minority, however, when it comes to dating or driving for teenagers. They all want to do these things. So the question I want to ask is:

Are there other things that all teenagers want to do and are those things connected in some way with learning?

Or, to put this another way, if school had been designed around something other than subjects, what would it have been designed around? Driving and dating, which we know are winners in a teenager's world, could be seen as subjects, or they could be seen as instances of something else, and that something else might be something important to learn.

Students everywhere might want to learn whatever that is and they would work hard to learn it. If we can turn the question around in that way, maybe we can design better learning situations for everybody.

So, the question is:

What are driving and dating instances of, with respect to learning?

Or, to address this from the cognitive science point of view:

What is it that students are doing when they learn to drive and date that they might be getting better at while doing those things?

Can we view whatever it is they are getting better at as an example of the kinds of things we should want to teach and that students should want to learn? Answering these questions will allow us to look at education in a new way. We need to think about how people actually learn, regardless of the subject, in order to address them.

Let's think about dating, then. I was never any good at it as a kid. I know how the non-cool guys feel. But, later on, much later on, I got very good at it. So, I must have learned something. What?

What was I bad at as a kid? Meeting girls, for one thing. Other kids could do it easily. I always needed to be fixed up.

Talking to girls, for another. I hardly knew any girls. I went to an all-boys high school. I was 16 when I went to college and the other freshmen were 18, so that didn't help either. In other words, I had no confidence.

But mostly, I had no idea what to say to a girl. What did they talk about?

And, one more thing. I really didn't get the point. I didn't know why one wanted to go out with girls anyway. I mean I eventually got the idea, at least I think I did.

Why am I saying it this way? I am trying to get an insight into the learning process and I am a fine example. I didn't know how to do it and then I did. I didn't get the point and then I did, sort of. So I must have learned something between the ages of 16 and 60. What?

Here are some things I learned:

- Human relationships are important, but they aren't easy to establish or maintain. They require work.
- The work involves, among other things, learning how to listen and respond to the needs of another human being. It involves subjugating one's own interests from time to time for the interests of another.
- Girls, and later women, feel good. Being with someone who loves you feels good. Learning to love feels good. More than feeling good, these things are critical for staying alive. This is not so obvious when you are surrounded by love from your family. But eventually you are alone, and alone is not so much fun.

As this is not a chapter on love, I will stop there. Suffice it to say that I learned how to meet girls, how to gain their interest, and how to form relationships with them. I also learned why I wanted to do that.

Now let's see what we have learned about learning from my little diversion into teenage angst.

We have learned that learning about how other people behave is very important.

We have learned that learning about one's own emotions and feelings is very important.

We have learned that building confidence is very important.

We have learned that learning to listen is very important.

We also have learned that learning how to express oneself is very important.

Now let's go back to discussing learning.

Why is it that teenagers are more interested in thinking about dating than they are in thinking about algebra? Why is it that they don't rate themselves on their success in dating in the same way as they do when they are discussing how they are doing in science?

What do teenagers know about learning that their school doesn't know?

This is it:

Teenagers know that the issues I have mentioned above will be important for them for the rest of their lives in a large variety of arenas, not just dating.

No matter what they do in life they will need to form relationships, assess their own abilities, gain confidence through practice, learn to listen, learn to love, try things out and see how well they work, and learn why they do what they do. To put this another way:

Dating is way more important than algebra and every teenager knows it.

Dating is much more important not because teenagers have raging hormones and they crave sex, as this phenomenon often is described. It is important because what they learn while dating serves them in many areas in life and relates strongly to who they will be and how well their lives will go.

Algebra relates to none of this and they know that too.

So, let me ask a simple question:

If we must have subjects in school, why wouldn't dating be rated as way more important than mathematics?

The answer to this is simple enough. School was not designed to help kids live better lives. That was never the point. But shouldn't it be?[2]

From a cognitive growth point of view, school wasn't even designed to teach us things that relate to learning per se.

Scholars designed the subject matter of the current school system. You hear sportscasters describe football players as *scholar-athletes*. Really? Scholars? Why would that be what we are seeking to create? There are only so many jobs for scholars, and while scholarship is very nice, it ought not be the goal we seek in school in a system of universal education.

Yes, but dating? Is that the subject I am proposing? Really?

Let me explain the real issue here. Take a look at the items I mentioned above.

> We have learned that learning about how other people behave is very important.
> We have learned that learning about one's own emotions and feelings is very important.
> We have learned that building confidence is very important.
> We have learned that learning to listen is very important.
> We also have learned that learning how to express oneself is very important.

Now, I will transform these slightly:

> Students need to learn about how other people behave and why, and they need to learn how to interact with different kinds of people.
> Students need to learn about their own emotions and feelings and how to deal with them.
> Students need to learn how to rely on themselves and feel confident in their own abilities.
> Students need to learn how to listen to others and really hear what they are saying.
> Students need to learn how to express themselves effectively.

Now this list doesn't seem so crazy, does it? In fact, most parents will tell you that they try very hard to teach all these things to their children. So one argument might be that the school doesn't have to do it, since parents do it.

Another argument might be that if the schools worked on these issues, they would have students memorize the 12 principles for building self-confidence and learn to express themselves by analyzing classics in world literature.

Here is the key point:

These issues, the ones that could be learned from dating, transcend all aspects of our lives.

And, more important, students know this. I started with the idea that learning begins with a goal. The points I listed above are goals that teenagers actually have. They would not have to be talked into those goals. Moreover those goals are, as all students know anyway, way more important than algebra. They aren't interested in becoming scholars.

Now let's consider the cognitive science behind this. Everything we do as human beings is goal-directed. We go for a walk for a reason, we shower for a reason, we get a job for a reason, we talk to people we meet for a reason. We pursue goals as soon as we are born. We try hard to learn to walk, talk, get along with our family, get our needs satisfied, and find out what we like and what we don't like. We do this from birth. If school related to the goals that children actually had, that they were working on at the very moment that they entered school, school would seem like a natural and helpful experience. Students wouldn't stress about satisfying their teachers any more than they stressed about satisfying their parents when they were learning to walk and talk. Yes, they want to please their parents, but that is not exactly the same thing.

People know what their goals are and they know when something they are being offered, a parasailing lesson or a pomegranate, for example, doesn't fit with their goals. They can be convinced to try out a new activity that they believe will not satisfy any of their goals, but for the most part it is difficult to convince them that weird things that were not on their goal list actually should be on the list. We say things to students like, "You will need this later." But this is usually a bold-faced lie. You don't need algebra later. Making up nonsense convinces nobody.

There is a more important issue here. Later on in this book I will detail the 12 kinds of learning that make up what it means to learn. If you get good at learning these things, you get good at what life has to offer. The list above is a partial list of the group of learning processes that I detail in Chapter 4. It is really quite important. I have used dating as a simple way of explaining it because no one has to explain why that matters to a teenager. Teenagers know that they have to learn the processes that I discuss in Chapter 4. As things are now, these important issues are not considered significant enough to deal with seriously in school. World history is always considered more important. But why should that be the choice?

Earlier, I mentioned that students want to learn how to drive as well as how to date. This is a pretty universal goal that teenagers have so we should ask of it as well whether it is important and what it might be an instance of that is inherently significant in real life.

On the surface, driving seems a skill that is an important part of daily life. So, one is led to ask why driving isn't a school subject? The answer is that it is. Driver's education has been taught in schools for many years. Not every school offers it, but many do. So what is the problem? It is just a useful skill, not a scholarly subject, so surely I am not suggesting that it is more important than physics. That is, of course, exactly what I am suggesting.

In our test-driven society, when driver's ed is taught, it is taught with a clear goal and a clear notion of success. When a student has passed the tests and gotten her driver's license, everyone is satisfied.

Well, not everyone. I was once called in on a consulting assignment for a university hospital that was working on a study to prevent teenage car accidents. The study was funded by an insurance company that would have been happy to pay out less in damages and, presumably, also thought fewer dead kids would be a generally good thing. What is the problem?

Students may have their licenses but they don't know much about driving and responsibility. It wouldn't be a shock to anyone to know that kids drink and drive, text message and drive, and generally yell and scream and goof around while driving. They often die from this behavior. Could we teach them not to do that? The answer always seems to be to put up posters that say don't drink and drive and to make them watch scary movies about car accidents. The school system strikes again.

If we tell them, then they will do it, never seems to work, but we keep trying.

I often have used the Department of Motor Vehicles (the DMV) as an example of the best there is in testing. They have two tests. Dumb multiple choice questions that make no sense and a real test that tests to see whether you can drive. Schools typically don't have the real test at all, one that tests to see whether you actually can do something, so the DMV at least is smarter than the school system.

But the real issue is something else entirely. Driving is an instance of a piece of very complex behavior that exemplifies one of the ways in which we learn. Perhaps more important, driving entails a great deal of other things, which could be learned and should be learned.

A simple example of this is car mechanics. Once upon a time schools taught kids to fix cars as well as to drive them. Perhaps they still do. But vocational subjects like that have been relegated to the back burner of education so that more testable subjects can be taught. Also, cars have gotten more difficult to fix. This is too bad, because if car mechanics were required instead of physics, students actually might learn science.

What do I mean by this?

When we hear an outcry about the nation's need to make children learn science, no one ever asks why. The standard answer, if this is ever asked, is that science is important in tomorrow's world or some such nonsense. Push harder and you might get some remarks along the lines that soon all the scientists will be Indian and Chinese, which may be the real fear of those who push science in the United States. To address this question properly, one has to ask what exactly is meant by "science."

Imagine that you are a student working on fixing a car in a car mechanics class. As I write this I am imagining a scene from the musical *Grease*, which was set in the 1950s when there actually were cars to work on in school. I never got to work on a car because I went to a science high school where such a thing would be looked down upon. So when I graduated from high school and drove to college and my car broke down, I hadn't the slightest idea what to do. I wish I could tell you that at least I understood the physics of the engine but I didn't. I just knew F = MA and other stuff that wasn't going to help me fix my engine.

Now let me ask you, how is fixing one's car engine like fixing one's air conditioning or plumbing? The answer to this question has embodied within it what it means to do science. When science means learning facts about science, we are talking about useless information that is readily forgotten after the test. I have no idea why anyone learns to balance chemical equations or apply physics formulas or learns about biology classifications in high school. None of this is of any use to most adults. (It is easy to test, however.)

When the stuff that is being taught does not relate to the inherent goals of the students, it will be forgotten. You can count on it. Why this stuff is taught is simply that it derives from a conception of science prevalent in the 1890s that has not been modified since. It is defended by people as a way to produce more scientists, which makes no sense since it probably deters more students from entering science than it encourages.

Scientific reasoning, on the other hand, *is* worth teaching.

Why?

Because car mechanics, plumbers, doctors, and crime investigators, to name four random professions, all do scientific reasoning on a daily basis. As a society we anoint only doctors with the glory of doing actual scientific reasoning. The other professions get less glamorous interpretations. But they are all doing the same stuff. This is what they are doing:

> They are taking a look at evidence and trying to determine the probable causes of the conditions that they have found.

To do this one must know what causes what in the real world, which is science; what counts as evidence of known conditions, which is science; and previous cases that are similar and that any good scientist must know. So while we may not think of a plumber as doing scientific reasoning, that is exactly what he is doing.

Science is about creating hypotheses and gathering evidence to support or refute those hypotheses. Children are natural scientists. They often try stuff out—skipping rocks on the water or dropping stones from the roof or lighting things on fire—to see what happens. But there is more to science than trying stuff out. One must seek explanations and make sure those explanations are correct. Knowing what constitutes a correct explanation is really the essence of what scientific knowledge is about. But notice that there are correct explanations for hypotheses in plumbing as well as in medicine and that these explanations exist for repairing a faulty engine and for understanding who committed a crime. It is all scientific reasoning.

The difference between plumbing and medicine is in the complexity of the science. Not a lot of invention goes on in plumbing and there aren't all that many explanations to choose from. The degree of difficulty in understanding what is going on and why is what separates those fields and makes one science and one not. But the basic thought processes are the same.

This is important to notice because all these areas of inquiry are what we might call diagnostic.

So, and this is the important part, the real issue from a cognitive science point of view is not in teaching science per se, but in teaching scientific activities, one of which is *diagnosis*. And, since diagnosis is a similar process no matter what you are diagnosing, it makes sense that all through school, diagnosis would be a subject, and not physics or literature. The things that children are asked to diagnose might start with things little kids like, like finding out what is wrong with their pets or their toys, and then move on to things bigger kids like, like cars and crime, and then move on to large issues, like why a business has failed or why our foreign policy doesn't work.

Diagnosis matters a great deal in our lives, yet it is not a subject in school. This is not surprising because the origins of the school subject areas, as I have said, are scholarly. But if we want to teach children to do things that matter and we want to retain their interest because they know intrinsically that these things do matter, then we must have them practice diagnosis all through their school lives, in a variety of venues that correlate with their interests. They don't all have to diagnose the same stuff. It is the diagnostic process itself that matters, not what is diagnosed.

I have been using the word *subject* for an idea like diagnosis but it is not a subject and should not be seen that way. I have been using the word only to contrast it to existing subjects in school. Diagnosis is a fundamental cognitive activity. Cavemen did diagnosis. They may not have done it well, but they did it well enough to continue the species. The diagnostic process is as old as people. Knowing why, being able to prove a hypothesis, is a fundamental cognitive process.

School needs to be organized around fundamental cognitive activities. It would be easy to demean what I have said here by saying

I want to teach kids to date and drive better. What kind of school is that?

But this trivializes the point. I do want to teach students to date and drive better. But these are just a few instantiations of general cognitive processes. Forming human relationships and figuring out what is going in the physical world are two of many very important cognitive abilities that manifest themselves in myriad ways in real life.

A properly designed school system needs to focus on cognitive abilities, not scholarly subjects. Kids will recognize instantly that these activities are the ones they know how to do and that they need to get better at. If we allow them to choose what areas of knowledge they would like to focus on while learning these skills, they would be attentive and interested students. No more ADHD. Poof!

A society that organized schools around cognitive abilities would become one where people were used to thinking about what they did and how and why they did it. They would not find school stressful or boring.

This wouldn't be a bad thing.

CHAPTER 2

Teaching Kids to Walk and Talk

Failure is instructive. The person who really thinks learns quite as much from his failures as from his successes.

—John Dewey

Teaching is a serious issue. Teachers matter. Or at least they should matter. But we have the sense that it is the job of the teacher to tell us stuff. Students expect it and teachers do it. Often, teachers get criticized if they do anything else. And, this is pretty much the beginning and the end of the problem with teaching. We force teachers to teach wrong.

I am beyond the age where I have little kids that I have to teach how to walk and talk. But when I did, I don't remember preparing any lesson plans. In a cognitive process-based model of education, all teaching looks like the teaching you do when you teach your children to walk and talk.

Lately I have been personally interested in being taught. This is because at the age of 55 I started to play softball in an old guys' softball league in Florida. I discovered I wasn't really very good. This was a bit surprising since I had played in the university softball leagues while I was a professor and had stopped playing only in my 40s. I wasn't a bad player then. There hadn't been that long a hiatus. And, I was playing against people a good deal older than myself since I am rather young as recent Florida transplants go. I used to be a good hitter and I wasn't now. The reason was easy enough to understand. In the university leagues they play fast pitch. A batter has a second or so to decide about swinging. It is all instinct. At least it was after having played for 40 some odd years.

But, in Florida, old guys play slow pitch. The pitcher throws the ball in a high looping arc and it is a strike if it lands on the plate. Quite a different experience from trying to hit a ball that is zinging by your head. Should be easier, no? Not for me. It took a bit of thinking to figure out why.

I analyzed how I was swinging, when I was swinging, and what kinds of pitches I was swinging at, and I came to many different conclusions. I realized I needed to wait longer before I swung. I realized I had to stop swinging at inside pitches (the ones that almost hit you). I realized that I had to stop swinging at pitches that looked good but yet dropped in front of my feet. I realized I had to see the ball hit the "sweet spot" on the bat. I realized I needed to change my whole approach to hitting, in fact.

OK. I realized a lot. I had come to many conclusions. Now what? Just do it, right? Aha. Not so simple.

You can't just do what you know you should do. Why not? Because your subconscious isn't listening to what you have to say. This is why you don't tell a little kid how to walk and talk. Apart from the fact that he wouldn't understand you anyway, even if he could understand you, the part of his mind that would be doing the understanding is the conscious part. Cognitive process-based teaching teaches nonconscious processes a good deal of the time.

A child learns a lot more from falling down than he ever will learn from hearing Mom say, "Watch your step."

We are wired to learn from failure. Those who don't learn from failure typically die young. We are descended from people who learned not to eat certain poisonous plants, and not to travel in a way that would expose them to danger, and to stay near their mates, and to protect their offspring. Those who didn't do these things, those who didn't learn from their own failures and from the failures of others, didn't get to have surviving offspring. The human race exists precisely because it is capable of learning from failure, both individually and collectively.

Did you ever wonder why what you learned in school isn't still in your head, or why you can't remember what your wife wanted you to get from the store on your way home? Or, why the things you have decided to do to improve your business or make more money or be a better person actually don't ever get executed? The answer is simple: You can't learn by listening—not from teachers, not from your wife, not from helpful suggestions from wise people, and not even from yourself.

Why not? Because it is your subconscious that is in charge of executing daily activities—from swinging a bat, to driving home, to talking to people you want to make an impression on, to getting along with your wife. Your conscious mind can make decisions, but your

subconscious pretty well does what it is in the habit of doing. The
subconscious is a habit-driven processor.

Bad habits, as they say, are hard to break. Actually, all habits, good
or bad, are hard to break. A new swing is really hard to develop, as is a
new way of selling, or a new way of treating people, or driving a new
route home.

This is the real use of education: the creation of new habits. This
can be done in only one way. The subconscious learns in only one
way.

The subconscious learns by repeated practice.

The only teaching that can work, then, is the kind of mentoring that
helps someone execute better while they are practicing.

How is a high school football coach different from a high school
history teacher?

Before we attempt to answer this question, we need to consider
why it is an important question to consider. In general, I think most
people would agree that the behavior of these two types of teachers is
likely to be quite different. In our mind's eye, we see images of yelling
and crude behavior versus refined lecture and discussion. But let's get
beyond the superficial stereotypes and think about what they teach
rather than their style of teaching it.

The history teacher at his worst teaches facts, and at his best teaches careful analysis of sources of facts.

The football coach at his worst teaches that someone could never
possibly do something, and at his best coaches someone to do something better.

The history teacher teaches the conscious. The football coach
teaches the subconscious.

This makes sense if we view education (in school) as a conscious
affair. It certainly seems to be a conscious affair. We discuss history,
we don't do history. And, it makes sense in football since the coach
doesn't need players who can discuss football—he needs players who
can execute.

It begins to make less sense when we consider how the conscious
and the subconscious interact.

As long as we see ourselves as rational beings who can think logically and make carefully reasoned decisions about our daily lives,
then education indeed should be about the promotion of reasoned

deliberation and the gaining of knowledge that will enhance our ability to reason. But suppose this conception we have of ourselves and our ability to reason logically is simply wrong?

Our entire education system depends on this debate. Actually the word *debate* is really not right here as there is no debate. The other side, the side that says we need to teach our unconscious because our conscious isn't capable of listening, has not really been expressed directly very often. It is, however, indirectly referred to often enough.

Plato comments:

> The most important part of education is right training in the nursery. The soul of the child in his play should be guided to the love of that sort of excellence in which when he grows up to manhood he will have to be perfected.

Why should this be the case? Why should it be in the nursery where real training takes place? And, what kind of training could the nursery provide—the kind of the football coach or the kind of the history teacher? And, what can we learn about education by considering seriously what Plato said?

The principles of learning in childhood are rather simple really. The first and most important part of an analysis of early childhood learning is an understanding of where the motivation comes from. If learning starts with a goal, as we have said, one question is, What goals do children have and how do they happen to have them?

When people mention motivation, the word *reward* often is added into the discussion. What kinds of rewards do children receive and to what extent are these involved in learning? Bear in mind that there are three kinds of rewards: intrinsic, extrinsic, and systemic. If it makes me happy, I don't need you to tell me I did well. If the activity doesn't really matter to me (an algebra test, for example), I will need some outside reward to even try. When do kids learn because of the use of external rewards? If I do well on an algebra test, it might be that it gives me intrinsic happiness to know I did well at algebra. As a math-oriented kid, I did get that kind of reward. It also makes you happy when your parents are proud of you. And it makes you happy when your grades win you admission into Yale or get you something else you might want. Which types of rewards figure into early childhood learning and what can we learn from this about learning? And, what will this tell us about teaching?

Let's start with walking and talking.

Walking and talking are intrinsically rewarding. No kid needs encouragement to do either. They do have to be discouraged from crying when a word will serve them better. *I want milk* works better than *wah.* But they learn this quite naturally without very much parental help. They learn to walk when their parents hold their hands and cheer when they succeed, but they would have learned to walk anyway.

The parents' role as the teachers of their children can be seen very clearly when we consider walking and talking. Kids can learn to do either without much help, but they do these things quicker and better   //
with parental help. Children who are spoken to by their parents, and listened to and corrected when they make an error, learn to speak well and more clearly as adults. While everyone learns to walk, parental care prevents falls when steps and other hazards present themselves.

So, is the parent teaching the child? What does the parent actually know about how to teach walking and talking? Actually the parent knows quite a bit about teaching. We are wired to teach our children and help them. All higher level animals do this as well. It is not a particularly conscious process.

So, at what point are children better taught by professional teachers instead of their parents? This is an important and interesting question.

A professional teacher is better than a parent if and only if the teacher knows more about what is being taught than the parent does. Teachers may take education courses and that may seem to qualify them to teach, but really those courses are not so much about the art of teaching per se. Teachers learn to teach by teaching, like anyone else learns how to do anything. But teachers learn to teach in the   ∨
system they find themselves in. This means that typically they learn how to manage classrooms and deal with administrators and handle various issues that are very specific to school.

Teaching outside of school usually does not entail managing multiple children nor should it entail dealing with state standards and other governmental interference (although that often happens anyway).

So, knowledge is the real issue in teaching, not teaching skill. Or so it would seem.

Actually this idea is clearly wrong if one thinks about university teaching. Professors become professors by writing a Ph.D. thesis, not by learning anything about teaching. They may have some teaching experience prior to becoming professors because they may have taught an introductory course or two as graduate students, but nobody teaches them how to teach. In fact, professors are not qualified to teach since they know nothing about teaching. They are hired by universities because of their research credentials, and teaching doesn't matter much. There is some lip service about the subject but no one ever got hired at Yale as a professor because she was a great teacher who did no research.

Here is a professor of computer science from a very highly ranked Big Ten university (he does not want his name mentioned):

> Every faculty member in the Department of Computer Science at my university thinks that their small insignificant area is important enough that all undergraduates must take a course in it. When you add all those courses up there is simply no time for a student to do anything other than take crazy courses in subdisciplines represented by the faculty in the department. Everybody's course is a sacred cow. If you tried to put something new in, something would have to come out, and no faculty member wants his course to be eliminated.

Professors are not there because they are good teachers.

I certainly knew nothing about teaching when I became a professor at Stanford many years ago. But I hated seeing students bored and miserable and started to think about what the problem was and how I could fix it. Many professors do exactly this. They want to be good at something they do regularly and their pride makes them into good teachers. Not all professors do this, by any means. What does it mean to become a good teacher in that context?

Professors are rated for their teaching ability. It is clear if one looks at those ratings what the criteria are from the students' perspective. They rate the friendliness, fairness, enthusiasm, and even the "hotness" of their teachers. These ratings have been studied extensively and conclusions like this one are typical:

> While student evaluations of faculty performance are a valid measure of student satisfaction with instruction, they are not by themselves a valid measure of teaching effectiveness. If student evaluations of faculty are included in the evaluation process of faculty members, then they should represent only one of many measures that are used.[1]

Professors and universities are very concerned about the evaluations of the teaching of the faculty and these days websites (like www.rate-myprofessors.com) make a very public show of how badly received some professors are. The professors are concerned with how they appear and whether they are liked and how all this might affect their salaries. They are not concerned with teaching effectiveness because they are not really teachers in their own minds.

Let's hear from an Ivy League professor (who also doesn't want to be named):

> There are faculty here who study real-world phenomena and don't know how to apply that knowledge to their own lives. We could teach students here how to make use of what we teach in their own lives, we just don't. Right now the approach that is taken makes most of the information that professors impart useless. It doesn't have to be that way.
>
> My colleagues here don't even do what they are studying when they are out of the lab. They are not successful people in life. If someone studying memory had to remember something, would they make use of their own data? I doubt it. Many of our professors don't realize that they may not know as much as they think they know. All these people assume that whatever they do is the best that can be done.

When a child learns to walk, you cannot say you were very good at teaching her to walk. She would have learned to walk without your help, most likely. When you teach a child to play baseball, you can more easily say that you were a good teacher, but really who knows you didn't screw him up with nonsense that it may take him years to undo? I was taught to step into the pitch in baseball and years later learned that what I was taught was wrong.

College professors can be evaluated on effectiveness only if someone knows what that means. Does it mean how well students do on exams? We can make easier exams then. Does it mean how many of them get into Ph.D. programs at Harvard or how many get good jobs upon graduation? That likely has nothing to do with the effectiveness of the professors.

There are no measures that make sense, for a very simple reason. College teaching doesn't make much sense in the first place. Lecturing and giving grades is certainly not a paradigm that any parent would use. You don't grade your child on speaking ability; you help her speak better. If it takes longer to do that, then it does. Even the DMV doesn't care about effective teaching. It doesn't give grades, just licenses. *Can you do it well?* is the question the DMV is charged with answering. But *can you do it well?* isn't a meaningful question in the top universities because there is typically nothing, other than research, that anyone is really being taught to do.

This leaves us in a quandary when it comes to understanding what it means to teach well. Here is the Ivy League professor again:

> People need to learn to generalize the information that they are given. They need to learn how to think about content in order to see how that content may or may not be true for them. We do not do that here. Instead we teach that this is the way it is done.
>
> We have kids at mediocre universities who don't know the facts and then we have kids at the good schools who know the facts but very few who know that those facts are not necessarily true. We need a different approach to knowledge than we currently have. By having students memorize the facts, it makes it seem as if the facts are truer than they actually are. We need to teach students to attack the facts and not to replace them with other facts.
>
> If facts are taught here in this way, and we are setting the standard, then we have a problem. Some faculty here actually do teach in this way, but it is not the main culture. Even the hard-core facts, like dates, are arguable. Students are not taught to use the information they have to question other information.

If we are teaching something where there are no performance measures, then effectiveness cannot be gauged. If the performance measurement is based on an exam, this likely would not reflect on the teacher's ability at all. Some students do well on exams and others don't, even though they all hear exactly the same lectures. And, when there are performance measures, it is not always clear that it was the teacher who was in any way responsible for the success of the students (or their failure).

So what is effective teaching?

If a teacher is better at teaching a child than a parent is, it must be because the teacher knows something the parent doesn't know or, at least, doesn't know how to teach. This makes the teacher more effective than the parent, but for very uninteresting reasons. You can't teach what you don't know, of course.

But knowledge alone is meaningless because teaching is not about the transfer of knowledge. I realize that a great many people think that this *is* what teaching is about; except if that were the issue, students wouldn't even think about rating their teachers on anything except how much they knew. And, by the way, that is about the last thing teachers are ever rated on.

For the most part, teachers are rated by students on how entertaining they are. But entertainment and teaching are really not particularly related. They are not unrelated because you can't get through to someone who has tuned you out. But you can entertain your students and get great ratings and still teach them nothing.

Here is the Big Ten professor again:

> At a big state university, which one would think has an obligation to supply training to the students of that state in a major field in which students can readily find employment, the faculty could care less about that and they only want to do graduate teaching. We teach courses that are modeled after courses in the professor training schools like Harvard and MIT. But how many professors do we need?
>
> Superstars who bring a lot of funding are very important in the university. The superstar system made sense when there were superstars. But today how many of these superstars have really big ideas? Does my school really have any superstars at all? I don't think so.
>
> The School of Education, where I am also on the faculty, has a research focus, which they do badly. Most of their students plan to be teachers. But they teach them the literature and not how to teach. It is the same situation as in computer science. They really want their students to become professors of education. They are not teaching teachers to teach because they don't care about that. They look down their noses at teacher preparation schools. Ninety-eight percent of their undergraduates

want to become teachers but the faculty are focusing on their graduate students. They don't teach the teachers. They do it, but it is not their focus.

The average professor of education here understands that he is supposed to teach teachers to teach but he gets evaluated on his research not on the quality of teachers who come out. It is a research university. How many dollars do you bring in? How much do you publish? Where would quality of teacher training fit in that model?

So, again, what exactly is effective teaching? Let's look at two of the longer versions of what my former Ph.D. students and former employees wrote to me when I asked about good teaching. These stories each need some context in order to be understood, and then I will comment.

The first story is from a Ph.D. student of mine who then continued to work with me for 30 more years.

> You were collecting key things teachers needed to know to do story curricula properly. Your contribution was "know when to lie to students." That triggered all kinds of discussion, pro and con, leading eventually to a longer, more explicit statement about knowing when to oversimplify, etc.
>
> Reflecting on it later, I realized that "know when to lie to students" was the right way to say it. The rephrased version was too reasonable. It didn't trigger any emotional reaction and re-evaluation. "Know when to lie" is a lie, but that's the point.

Why is this story important? I placed it here because it reflects an important belief that I hold about teaching. At the moment to which he is referring, we were writing, as a group, a set of guidelines on how to teach Socratically using the online curricula we were building for high schools. We were, in essence, writing an instruction manual for teachers on how to teach in a new way. When I supervise very smart people who know perfectly well how to do things, I deliberately provoke them. I believe that my job is to make them think. There is no better way to make people think than by annoying them in a way that makes them defend their point of view, especially when their point of view may not have been well thought out.

It is important, when teaching Socratically, which is my preferred methodology, to make students question their beliefs. No one is a better teacher than a teacher who makes students wonder whether he has been wrong about something.

Do I think that teachers should lie to students?

I think teachers should make students think harder than they might have been capable of doing without the teachers. I also think that teachers should not tell answers to students. Students do not learn from memorizing answers. They learn from developing questions for themselves that they then can begin to find answers to.

I believe that effective teaching makes . . .

students develop questions to which they then will seek answers
students look for answers from people other than the teacher
students confused and less certain than they were before

Now, I realize that these are pretty nonstandard ideas. That is, of course, the point.

This next writer worked for me (after getting his Ph.D. elsewhere) in the academic world and later in the business world.

Probably the most important lesson I learned from you was the value of overstatement and oversimplification in communicating ideas and getting people's attention. I recently retired and was roasted at my retirement party by a group of longtime employees and there were some interesting anecdotes about what I'd taught them about selling their ideas through management. Software engineers are often uncomfortable making a point without giving every possible nuance, caveat, and detail. This typically causes management's eyes to gloss over and their ideas never get a fair hearing. So, I've (apparently relentlessly) encouraged employees to make their points quickly and to use overstatement and oversimplification as rhetorical devices. I'm still wincing over the roasts that portrayed my predilection for interrupting presenters and asking, "What's your point?"—I learned that one from you.

I most certainly taught the lessons this writer describes. I hated it when students couldn't get to the point, and I frequently interrupted them when they were speaking. In business, I make a point of saying things that are very simple, which tends to upset people. I find this a good way to start a conversation that addresses complex issues.

Of course, I never actually say any of this. I simply do it. The real issue in teaching, by parents or by teachers or by anyone else, is the model you present to the students. That model is presented by what they see you do and how they see you act. They can choose to emulate you or not. But a good teacher makes students think about how to behave and about what works and what doesn't.

I believe that effective teaching makes . . .

students think about how the teacher is behaving and causes
the students to wonder about whether copying this behavior
would be a good idea
students think about what works and what doesn't in the adult
world

This next writer is a professor at a major university. I hired him to be on the faculty at Yale, which was his first academic job.

I teach by telling stories that are meaningful to me. I let them see who I am and how I live. I let them see what is important to me and why. To be a real teacher you have to let yourself be vulnerable. The student needs to see that you are a human with feelings and fears and goals. You are saying to students: This is the way I do it; it fits with who I am; it helps me be successful; and don't let anyone tell you that you can't do something. Everyone wants to control you, but in the end, you have to be you, for better or worse. So, don't let anyone tell you that you can't do something.

I tell that story over and over and over again in different ways. About my research, about my company, about my family. I walk the talk.

And, the students have to see that there are consequences of breaking the rules; that it costs; and the costs can be high at times. But that's part of the price of believing in yourself. Sometimes you get hurt and then you have to pick yourself up and try it again.

This writer was writing about his teaching. I behave this way as well, and he knows it.

I believe that effective teaching makes . . .

students think about the stories the teacher tells
students believe that their teacher is not a phony, so they can
take what is said seriously
students think about what it means to put oneself on the line for
one's own beliefs

The next writer worked for me as a writer for many years. Her main career was, and is, as a concert musician.

My high school English teacher was a great teacher. He was married to the Singer sewing machine heiress but committed to teaching kids. He had us keep a writing journal and was just excellent at helping me understand what was so personal to me that others wouldn't be able to connect (or perhaps just plain sappy romantic drivel!) and what was "strong" and pertinent to everyone. I still have the journal and wince at what I wrote but still really admire his comments in the margins.

In the future, in a world where online learning begins to preempt classroom teaching, mentoring will replace lecturing. Many teachers know how to mentor but often they are not given the opportunity or don't take the time to do it. The teacher described above was a personal writing mentor, which is about the only way you can teach someone to write.

I believe that effective teaching makes . . .

students look more carefully at the work that they themselves
have produced
students believe that their teacher is their personal mentor

Here is the same woman, this time writing about how she learned music.

> My mentor, Otto-Werner Mueller, was conducting the Yale Philharmonia in the 1970s—I met him as an undergrad in Madison, WI. I attended his graduate seminars in Madison and spent a lot of time with him while he was in New Haven. He guest-conducted the Hartford Symphony (where I now work) twice in the past few years. (He is 83 now.) I spent hours and hours in "lab orchestra" watching him teach his conducting students, both in Madison and at Yale. What always struck me was how students were either so self-conscious they were wooden, or how they'd try to imitate Otto (who at 6 feet, 7 inches had amazing stature) physically and couldn't pull it off. Very few were able to incorporate what he was teaching and then make it their own.

> I believe that effective teaching makes . . .

> students look at what the teacher does and see how they can
>   imitate it in a way that is consonant with who they are

The next writer was a Ph.D. student of mine and is now a professor at a major university.

> Trust your intuitions. This was something you told many of us over and over. It has had three meanings for me—first, that the only right things to work on are those that I can imagine a solution to; second, that whether a way of attacking something is the right way or not, it will lead me to the right way; and third, go out on a limb. I can't say how I learned this except, perhaps, through trusting your advice and then noticing that it got me to success over and over again. It began to really sink in when I had my own students. Often, the most interesting things they brought to me were more intuitive than they were based on what everyone else was saying. And I have had to reassure people that their ideas are good and they should follow up on them. Of course, there are also intuitions that my students have that I don't think are good, and I don't advise them to follow

up on those. So I think I now believe in trusting intuitions that someone I trust can also see value in, and for my students, trust intuitions that someone they trust can also see value in.

I believe that effective teaching makes . . .

students trust their own intuitions
students trust their teacher's advice

The final two are a little different from the others. I included them because teaching is not always implicit, as the above stories indicate, but sometimes explicit. The next writer was student of mine who is now high up in a large corporation.

You taught me that you always start by collecting data—so basic, but so often overlooked. I recall watching most of your papers start by collection of data. I recall watching your criticisms of work that was just abstraction on abstraction, with no data at its roots. For the work I'm currently doing, I have a log of all the types of entities (typically business or government enterprises), interactions (typically business models or sustainability models), and outcomes. I just gave five talks last week and used the method of "start by collecting data" when introducing my work and when being a critical thinker about the work of others that was being presented to me.

This point is about how to do real research does not apply to everyone. But a more general form of this advice is to start at the beginning, which is usually useful advice. Knowing where the beginning is can be complicated, however.

I believe that effective teaching makes . . .

students understand how to begin a process
students understand what you tell if you constantly demonstrate
the value of what you tell them

This writer was another of my Ph.D. students who is now a professor at a major university.

You taught me about the important role of explicit social hierarchies in a learning environment. At Yale the hierarchy was very clear and everyone knew exactly where they stood. You pay your dues before you join the club and academia is chock full of clubs. You taught this by both example and explanation. Seeing a good clear example of a social hierarchy that works (such as the one we had in our lab at Yale) gave me one level of understanding, but I had to see what happens when the hierarchy is not so obvious to truly appreciate the importance of the whole concept. Any longstanding community will have a social hierarchy, but it's not always so obvious (especially when the community likes to pretend it doesn't exist), and that makes it really hard on newcomers. I've seen some really stellar junior faculty get into difficult tenure decisions because no one was guiding them politically (or else they just blew it off). And more recently I've been running into more and more students with "entitlement issues" who just don't seem to buy into any social hierarchies. There is a lot of social commentary on why this is happening and how the workplace needs to adjust to a whole generation of kids who always got trophies.

I believe that effective teaching makes . . .

students understand where they fit in the world in which they live
students understand how to get ahead in the world in which they live
students understand the roles of those around them

There is certainly a great deal more that one could say about effective teaching. Unfortunately, much has been written on effective teaching that is not particularly helpful. Mostly it is politically correct advice that is quite difficult to implement. Here are two lists that I found. The first is from Learning to Teach in Higher Education.

1: Interest and explanation
2: Concern and respect for students and student learning
3: Appropriate assessment and feedback

4: Clear goals and intellectual challenge
5: Independence, control, and active engagement
6: Learning from students

The second is from a Michigan State website and was taken from a book by Arthur W. Chickering and Zelda F. Gamson entitled *Seven Principles for Good Practice in Undergraduate Education.*[2]

Principle 1: Good practice encourages student–faculty contact
Principle 2: Good practice encourages cooperation among students
Principle 3: Good practice encourages active learning
Principle 4: Good practice gives prompt feedback
Principle 5: Good practice emphasizes time on task
Principle 6: Good practice communicates high expectations
Principle 7: Good practice respects diverse talents and ways of learning[3]

Whenever I see phrases like *diverse talents* or *ways of learning* or *active learning* or *active engagement* I am very distrustful of the advice being offered. *Active learning* should mean learning by doing, but it never does because learning by doing is very difficult to implement in the university context (which is where this advice comes from). It is easier to do it in 1st grade, but after a while the class has to sit still and listen and that is not active learning no matter what the teaching guides say. *Different learning styles* is usually a way of saying, "some people are dumber than others," which no one wants to say. What bothers me most about these kinds of lists is that they avoid saying what really needs to be said. It is nearly impossible to measure your success as an effective teacher because the performance expectations of students are almost always about test scores and very rarely about actual production.

With this idea in mind, that effective teaching means helping students do what it is they wanted to do and not what it is that you wanted them to do, I will list the suggestions I have been scattering about in this chapter. Bear in mind that this is not meant to be a complete list. I got this list the way you saw, by interpreting things written by students and former employees about their own experiences.

Effective teaching makes . . .

students develop questions to which they then will seek
    answers
students look for answers from people other than the teacher
students confused and less certain than they were before
students think about how the teacher is behaving and causes
        the students to wonder about whether copying this behavior
        would be a good idea
students think about what works and what doesn't in the adult
        world
students think about the stories the teacher tells
students believe that their teacher is not a phony, so they can
        take what is said seriously
students think about what it means to put oneself on the line for
        one's own beliefs
students look more carefully at the work that they themselves
        have produced
students believe that their teacher is their personal mentor
students look at what the teacher does and see how they can
        imitate it in a way that is consonant with who they are
students trust their own intuitions
students trust their teacher's advice
students understand how to begin a process
students understand what you tell if you constantly demonstrate
        the value of what you tell them
students understand where they fit in the world in which they live
students understand how to get ahead in the world in which
        they live
students understand the roles of those around them

Now, taking my own advice about starting with the data and then clas-
sifying it, let's look at these rules as a group. What exactly are they suggestions about? Broadly speaking, they fall into the following categories:

Helping students think:

students develop questions to which they then will seek
    answers
students look for answers from people other than the teacher

students are confused and less certain than they were before
students think about the stories the teacher tells

Helping students observe and copy good behavior:

students think about how the teacher is behaving and wonder
 about whether copying this behavior would be a good idea
students think about what works and what doesn't in the adult
 world
students look at what the teacher does and see how they can
 imitate it in a way that is consonant with who they are

Making students respect their advisors:

students believe that their teacher is not a phony, so they can
 take what is said seriously
students believe that their teacher is their personal mentor
students trust their teacher's advice
students understand what you tell if you constantly demonstrate
 the value of what you tell them

Teaching students how and when to take action:

students think about what it means to put oneself on the line for
 one's own beliefs
students understand how to begin a process

Teaching students to be good critics of their own work:

students look more carefully at the work that they themselves
 have produced
students trust their own intuitions

Teaching students their place in the world and how to succeed
in that world:

students understand where they fit in the world in which they live
students understand how to get ahead in the world in which
 they live
students understand the roles of those around them

Effective teaching, then, means teaching these things:

How to be a critic
Whom to respect and copy
How to know where you fit
How to take action
How to think

The relevant question for a teacher, then, is: Does your teaching result in students who can do the five things listed above? There are many ways to get those things to happen for students. These, however, typically do not include lecturing, being entertaining, giving easy grades or easy tests, or marching students through boring exercises that teach them the truth.

Effective teaching is made much easier, of course, if what you are trying to teach is something worth learning. So, let's move on to discussing that.

CHAPTER 3

What Can't You Teach?

Nothing in education is so astonishing as the amount of ignorance it accumulates in the form of inert facts.

—Henry B. Adams

When children are born, they come with distinct personalities. Ask any mother of a second child. "It even behaved differently in the womb," she will say. One kid is aggressive while the other is contemplative. One kid is constantly talking while the other hardly says a word. One kid is shy while the other is outgoing.

Often, when we think about teaching and learning, we have the idea that if we want someone to do something, or know something, or behave in a certain way, all we have to do is teach it to them. So we teach kids to appreciate music, when they may have no interest in, or inclinations toward, music at all, or to act in the class play, when they are simply bad at acting, or to throw a baseball when they simply can't do it and don't care. Often, but not always, we are forgiving of the differences between people and their individual talents, and we acknowledge that she is tone deaf, or he will always throw poorly, and we give up.

Small children are like sponges. They ask questions constantly and, if they have reasonable parents, get answers. The belief system that children adopt is usually quite similar to that of their parents. They don't decide to try out a different religion at age 5; they do what they have always known. They eat what they were fed and they like to go to places they have been taken. Parents influence every aspect of a child's belief system. Because of that, we have the sense that we can teach children anything, but this gets less true as they get older. The Jesuits have a saying about teaching a child before he is 7 and thus producing the man he will become. There is some truth to this. If you really learn honesty when you are 5, it is unlikely you will become a crook. Your subconscious wouldn't permit it.

Then, what is the role of the subconscious here? When a child is being taught at 3, he is not being taught consciously. He does not memorize rules for walking or talking and he does not learn anything very much by consciously trying to learn. Rather, a child absorbs by constantly practicing and then making that practice a part of who she is.

Later, when the subconscious attitudes about walking, talking, relating to others, family values, and all the rest, are well within the deep subconscious of the child, we begin the attempt to teach the child consciously. We worry when we hear, for example, that:

> About a quarter of teens questioned in the broad survey weren't able to correctly identify Adolph Hitler as Germany's chancellor during World War II. About 20 percent couldn't say whom America fought in that war.[1]

More than a quarter wrongly believed Columbus sailed to the New World after 1750. Half didn't know whom Senator Joseph McCarthy investigated. And a third had no clue the Bill of Rights is the source of freedoms of religion and speech. Nearly a third couldn't tell you who said in a famous speech: "Ask not what your country can do for you . . . ."

Until a child enters school, he has been learning things that are useful to him. He knows where his toys are and how to play with them; he knows how to get food; he knows how to get his parents to do what he wants (perhaps); he knows how to entertain himself. In short, he has learned what he has learned because he has found his new abilities to be of value.

And the history cited above? Of what value is it to know about Joe McCarthy? Not only is it of no value to a child, but what we know about McCarthy is slanted by whoever is writing the history and biased by whatever point the person is trying to make. It is all very well to tell students the truth about what happened in the past and assume that they will learn from it, and therefore not repeat it, but we can't easily know the truth and they are not likely to learn much from the telling anyhow.

Pundits scream and yell about what children don't know. The question is: Why do they need to know it? If the answer is that it makes the system happy that they know certain facts while not making the child in any way happier, we all can guess how well that is going to turn out.

The bottom line here is one of initial belief systems and fundamental personality characteristics, coupled with the notion of truly held goals. You cannot teach someone something that:

- does not help them achieve some goal they actually hold
- is not in line with their fundamental personality characteristics
- goes against their subconscious beliefs

You can try, but you won't succeed.

So the question of what you can't teach, which is very important when we think about teaching and learning, comes down to a question of whom the child has become because of what she learned prior to the age of 7, and what she was anyway when she exited the womb. Those two things are powerful enough even if you don't add in trying to teach something that in no way relates to any goal the child has.

This is even more true for adults, of course. We can try to teach adults things that are at odds with who they are as people, but good luck with that.

Traits may come with the child, or they may have been learned by the child prior to the age of 7, but it really makes no difference when we are discussing teaching. Personality cannot be changed. Core beliefs are very hard to change. Interests are hard to change, although new ones can be found. Clinical psychologists try to make small changes in these aspects of people but they have a very difficult time doing it.

But my point here is to address an issue in education and training that is not well understood. Simply stated it is this: *It is not possible to teach or train students to do things that are not in line with who they are as people.* This matters because much of what we try to teach in school and train for in companies is an attempt to alter behavior.

I have been building what have come to be called e-learning systems for about 25 years. Over the years, I have realized that there is nothing new under the sun in the subject matter that e-learning systems are asked to address. One of my least favorite subjects, one that comes up frequently, is integrity and compliance. I have been asked to work on this subject quite often. Usually what is being asked is impossible. Most e-learning companies simply do what they are asked to do by the client without pointing out—if they even know—that what they are being asked to teach can't be taught. Companies that need to train their employees in such things, because of some regulation or other, ask for it, and e-learning companies willingly build it.

Unfortunately, as my mother would have attested to, were she still around, I was born with off-the-scale honesty. I can't build e-learning I know won't work any more than I was able, when I was 5, to let my mother walk out of a store without paying (by mistake) without becoming hysterical.

So, now I am hysterical about fraudulent education and fraudulent e-learning—namely, courses that claim to teach subjects that alter the very nature of a person. Of course, such courses don't say that is what they are trying to do, but it is pretty much the basis of courses about safe driving or drugs or sexual behavior, or how not to violate the law.

How is training about compliance an attempt to alter basic behavior?

Recently I was presented with an opportunity to teach integrity and compliance to the employees of a large company that bids on RFPs. The bidding process is part of a legal process and the company wants its employees to stay within the guidelines.

Fair enough. Makes sense.

Except, when you look at the guidelines, they include an array of rules spelled out in a complex document, typically a signed legal contract for potential bidders. To know those rules, one would have to read the contract. In effect, the company wants to train people to read, and pay careful attention to, the contract. The company wants to do this by putting employees in fictitious situations in which someone has not read the contract, and this failure to read causes serious difficulties for the company when the employee violates a rule he didn't know about.

Much of e-learning is like this. You are the manager of a large project, which needs to finish on time, and is over budget. Do you:

- steal money
- lie about the time you have spent
- tell the company it can keep the damn project
- carefully explain to your superiors the problems that exist and let them decide

Do people learn from stuff like this? Of course not. But everyone feels better after producing it. At least I assume they do.

If this stuff makes people happy, then build more of it, by all means. But if we want to address real issues, we need to discuss personality and how to deal with it.

I have insisted, as long as I have been discussing education,[2] that learning has to be experientially based. I proposed building complex social simulators 20 years ago, and this has come to be understood by the e-learning community as telling people they are in a situation that they may or may not relate to instead of actually putting them into a very realistic simulation of that situation. The reason they do it that way is money, of course, but something gets lost in the translation.

What is the difference?

Suppose that I tell you that you are a baseball player in the major leagues and your team is down by one run with one out in the bottom of the ninth with the bases loaded. I then give you a set of multiple choices about what to do on the first pitch (like, a—take the first pitch, b—look for a fast ball, etc.). What is the problem with this? There are right answers about what to do, but they depend on many variables (Do you know this pitcher's habits? How have you been hitting today? How fast is the guy on third?). Pretending that we can abstract a situation with a simple description and then suggest there is a right answer, is absurd. But more important, if you have never actually been in that situation, if you have never played baseball, your comprehension of the unmentioned details is likely to be zero. Attempting to teach anything through short descriptions of situations followed by multiple choice answers is just dumb.

Why, then, do e-learning companies keep on building courses that sound like that? Usually the answer is that corporations that don't know any better asked them to.

What does this have to do with altering basic behavior? I do indeed play baseball, as I have said, and what I would do in that situation depends on my personality in many ways. It also depends on an accurate assessment of my own abilities. What it doesn't depend on is deep thought. Professional athletes do not become professional athletes owing to their superior cognitive abilities. They have superior physical abilities and rely on instinct for thinking. They do what they "know" to do. They don't think it out. Coaches try like crazy to get them to think it out, but you often can find a 20-year professional veteran getting chewed out by his coach and being asked, What were you thinking? Nothing. He was thinking nothing. Correct action is rarely about thought, especially when little time for thinking is available.

So, then, how do we teach people to do the right thing, especially when the right thing is not in line with their normal behavior?

Can we teach nurturance, or aggression, or extroversion, or orderliness? I hope that it is obvious that we cannot do this. People are born with these characteristics. They are not learned. Ask any parents of more than one child. They will respond that their children had certain personality traits that were apparent from birth. My grandson Milo is a neatnik. Everything has to be in its place. Also, he loves to perform in front of an audience. His parents do not share and did not teach him these behaviors. The degree to which we have such traits defines our innate personalities. So, we need to translate this question into one we can answer.

The real issue is one of degree and not of kind. You will never teach someone who is fundamentally dishonest to be very honest, or vice versa. You will never teach someone who is very aggressive to be very passive. What you can do is make people aware of the consequences of their actions and hope to change their behavior slightly, when they have the time to think about what they are about to do. You can make people aware of their behavior, and their rational selves can direct what they do, if they have time to think about. But their subconscious is likely to want them to behave differently, and it is their subconscious that is usually in charge in a pinch.

Someone who hates details is not a good candidate for being taught to read contracts in detail. Similarly, someone who loves details is not a great candidate for sales rep. (Why? Because being very people-oriented is actually a characteristic that never goes hand in hand with being detail-oriented.) So, it is not uncommon for companies to be faced with the arduous task of training their salespeople to pay attention to detail. Telling them to hire differently is hopeless, because people who are both very detail-oriented and love engaging people socially do not exist. Accountants don't usually win personality contests. What to do?

This is indeed a job for teaching but not for teaching of the usual sort. To see what kind of job it is, we need to think for a moment about how the mind works. Specifically, we need to think about how the unconscious learns to make decisions.

If you have a character trait, say, honesty, you have had to come to grips over the years with its upside and its downside. People appreciate you for being honest, but not when they ask you if they look good after they have spent an hour dressing. (I speak from experience here.) People dislike dishonesty but not when it helps get a deal closed because you said you loved a restaurant that you really hated. We have mixed feelings about honesty, as we do about any personality characteristic. We like friendly people but we dislike overly friendly people. Who decides which is which is anybody's guess. Teenagers often try to be all things to all people, but as adults they soon realize that they simply will have to be themselves and they will try to find work and friends that suit the personalities that they happen to have.

Personality features are not conscious. We don't decide which ones to have, and we may not even be aware of how others perceive us. We do what we feel comfortable doing and we push on. And then we meet integrity and compliance officers.

They tell us to read every detail of a contract to make sure we are in compliance, and those who are detail-oriented and fearful of making errors and introverted and sensitive do it without question, and those people who are gregarious and confident and aggressive figure they can get by without it. What is an integrity and compliance officer to do?

Here is what not to do:

- Don't try to tell people who naturally act one way to act differently.
- Don't make a movie of the idiot who did it wrong and say, See, look how dumb that guy was and look what trouble he got into.
- Don't lecture on the benefits of behaving the way the company wants you to behave.
- Don't write a manual with correct behavior that no one will read.
- Don't build an e-learning course with multiple choice answers where one of them is the right thing to do.

The mind is organized around experiences. We remember our experiences and we index our remembered experiences so that we can find them later. Individuals don't know how they do this, but cognitive science can tell something about how this process works. You can't find an experience that was indexed wrong, for example.

Good indexing involves figuring out the goal that an experience relates to and the conditions that allowed that goal to be achieved or not. We do not do this consciously. We learn by doing, that is, we learn from experience, and from thinking about those experiences. When we have understood our experiences well enough, we can (unconsciously) index them so that they will come up again just in time when we need them again. (This is what we call being reminded.) It is beyond the scope of this book to explain how that process works.[3] The simple idea is that experiences get labeled when we think about them and not otherwise.

So the real question for an integrity and compliance officer is how to get people to think about integrity and compliance issues. This thinking needs be done over time in a complex way and voluntarily. How might we do that?

That is the real question.

One answer to this is stories. People really like stories. As long as there have been people, there have been stories; we have moved from epic poems and theatre to novels and movies in recent years, but, by and large, the stories are the same. How to overcome obstacles to getting what you want, is a theme that dominates much of literature, for example. Movie makers say it as "boy meets girl, boy gets girl, boy loses girl, boy gets girl." There have been many books written about the basic plots that occur again and again in stories.

Human beings understand stories because stories resonate with them. Characters have dilemmas that readers or viewers themselves have had. Stories appeal to emotions rather than logic, and emotions are at the heart of our pre-7-year-old unconscious selves. We feel something because of a well-told story and that feeling can help us see something in a new way.

Why am I going on and on about stories? I believe that all of human intercourse is about the exchange of stories. (I wrote a book about this.[4]) If you want to appeal to the pre-7-year-old unconscious that resides in all of us, you need to hit emotion not logic. This means that a good story can help someone to reconsider deep down in their unconscious a feeling or attitude or seemingly immutable personality trait that they can feel perhaps is somewhat dysfunctional. Stories can change our natural instincts.

That story cannot be short and sweet. It takes a great deal of emotion and empathy to change a point of view in a belief system. Deciding to construct a 15-minute, e-learning module in which one plays the sales rep and learns that honesty is the best policy, is so absurd that I am sorry I am referring to it at all, except that is what was proposed by the integrity and compliance people to whom I was speaking.

You can move people ever so slightly by having them have emotional experiences that they can discuss with one another. Imagine a book club that deals with a book about dishonesty and causes people in the discussion group to talk about the subject. If the book presented deep dilemmas to which there were no obviously right answers, this would allow people to get to and discuss their unconscious beliefs. Simply articulating those beliefs can be quite helpful. This is what clinical psychologists are really trying to do, after all. It is also what literature professors are trying to get their classes to do. Thinking about and talking about complex emotional issues makes personality traits and core beliefs something you can think about consciously.

The real issue, in the end, is interests. Teaching works best when you teach students who agree that they really want to learn whatever it is you have to teach. This means making sure that students are preparing to do things that they want to do and actually will do. That makes teaching much easier for all involved. The one-size-fits-all curriculum doesn't work because one size doesn't fit all. Let detail-oriented people learn detailed kinds of things. Let artistic people learn artistic kinds of things. Let logical people learn logical kinds of things. Everyone would be much happier and all would enjoy learning a lot more if we simply let people be themselves.

CHAPTER 4

Twelve Cognitive Processes That Underlie Learning

Those who know how to think need no teachers.
—Mahatma Gandhi

Not everything we would like to teach can be taught, as we have seen. Similarly, not everything we would like to learn can be learned, especially if we are taking the wrong approach to learning. In the previous chapter we discussed what can't be taught. Now, let's talk about what can be taught.

One problem in such a discussion is that we are used to (because we went to school) thinking about what needs to be taught and learned in terms of subjects (English, math, science, etc.). We think this way because school originally was organized by professors who had specialties in these subject areas. These professors were scholars and they set up the lower schools on the basis of the specialties that they had.

When I was working in artificial intelligence, I began to realize that what I needed to teach the computer to do in order for it be smart was a far cry from what people thought needed to be taught. People assumed that we needed to tell the computer facts about the world of the type that children learn in school, and that this would make the machine smart. (Quite recently, I attended a meeting of AI people who were planning a project to allow computers to pass SAT tests as a way of showing that the computer was smart!)

But what computers lack is intelligent capabilities, not information. It is easy enough to fill a machine with information, but when you are done, it would be able to tell you only what you told it. (If that was what a child did, you would think that he was brain damaged.) Intelligence and the learning required to create useful new knowledge are really a result of an amalgamation of cognitive processes. Intelligent computers, and intelligent people, need those processes to be working well.

What I mean by this, is that there is stuff we can do mentally, and that learning just means doing that stuff and getting better at it. Learning is not any one process, but many processes, depending on what you are learning.

What are the cognitive processes that make up learning? If we wish to teach people, it is important to ask what cognitive capabilities we want them to have when we are done, not what we want them to know. In other words, we want to understand what we have to do in order to make them better able to think.

In this chapter, we will discuss the kinds of cognitive processes that people can (and must) learn to do well. Later we will discuss how to best approach learning and teaching these processes.

There are 12 types of processes outlined here. There may be more types than these, but with these we pretty much can cover the ground of what human learning looks like. I have divided them into three groups: *conceptual processes*, *analytic processes*, and *social processes*. Notice first that all the types are types of processes. Thinking is a process. It is something we do. We need to see what that doing is like.

All these processes require practice in order to master them. You cannot learn to master a process without practicing it again and again. Feedback and coaching help one learn.

CONCEPTUAL PROCESSES

1. Prediction: Making a prediction about the outcome of actions

This is experiential learning about everyday behavior in its most common form—it includes learning about how to travel or eat or get a date, for example. In its complex form it is how one learns to be a battlefield commander or a horse race handicapper. One learns through experience by trial and error. The cognitive issue is building up a large case base and indexing that case base according to expectation failures, as I described in *Dynamic Memory*. We learn when predictions fail. When they succeed, we fail to care about them because most of the predictions we make are uninteresting (I predict the room I just left will look the same when I return). Learning to predict what will happen next requires repeated practice in each domain of knowledge.

There is some transfer across domains but not that much. (Learning to buy an airplane ticket is somewhat related to eating in a restaurant, but not that closely. You might use a credit card in each, for example, and might be refused service because you are rude.)

2. Modeling: Building a conscious model of a process

We need to learn how things work. A citizen knows, presumably, how voting works. Someone looking for venture capital should know how fundraising works. Processes need to be learned in order to effectively participate in them and in order to propose changes in them. Building a conscious model of a process matters a great deal if you want to make the process work for you. If you want to get into college, you need to understand how the process works. This cannot be learned from experience in a serious way because one may do it only once and may not be able to experience the entire process. Having the process explained to you may not work that well either because this will not bring an operational understanding of it (as opposed to a more superficial understanding of it). Designing it, modifying it, and participating in simulations of it work much better as learning methods.

3. Experimentation: Experimentation and replanning based on success and failure

This is probably the most important learning process we engage in while living our lives. We make life decisions and we need to know when we need to change something. There are big decisions—like getting married or how to raise a child or whether to change jobs—and little decisions, such as changing your diet or your sleep habits. We make our decisions on the basis of what has worked before and what has failed to work. We tend to make life decisions without much knowledge. We don't know how our bodies work all that well and we don't really know how the world works or what it has in store for us. Thinking about these issues and learning from failure is a pressing need all through life. Learning to analyze what has worked out and what has not and why is part of living a rational life. These things can be learned by living and talking about our experiences, thus creating a database of stories that we can rely on later. We learn by talking with others and hearing their stories, but we also learn from our own experience as we construct our own stories. We can learn about life experiences through reading and movies as well. We like stories in all these forms precisely because they focus on real-life issues. The cognitive task here is story creation, comparison, indexing, and modification. Most conversation depends on story exchange. The more emotional a story is, the more likely it is to be remembered.

4. Evaluation: Improving our ability to determine the value of something on many different dimensions

There are no rights and wrongs in what we like. But there is general agreement about what makes a work of art great. The factors to be considered are not necessarily conscious, although for experts they typically are. In these more subjective and subconscious areas of life, it is more a matter of trying to understand what feels right than understanding why it feels right. There is a difference between being someone who can make an artistic judgment and being an art expert. One might learn to notice things that one had failed to notice, if someone takes the time to point them out. Learning to make artistic judgments is about learning to notice, to describe, and to appreciate. One's concept of beauty changes when one's focus changes. Practice is a key idea here as is the assembling of a case base to use as a comparison set. Nevertheless, the comparison set is not usually conscious. One can like something because it is pleasing without realizing (or caring about) why it is pleasing.

When we make a value judgment, we don't necessarily know the values we have and we haven't necessarily learned them consciously. We should value human life over property but whether we do or not we will find out only if the situation arises. It is tempting to try to teach values but this actually is done so early in life and in so many subtle ways that anybody over the age of 10 is unlikely to be much affected by what people say to them about what they should value and what they shouldn't. Perhaps husbands should value helping their wives over watching football but that doesn't mean they will. In important areas of life, on the job and in child raising, for example, one's values come into play. If parents believe they shouldn't correct a child when he makes a mistake in speaking, they soon will find that they have a child who speaks poorly. The value held by the parents may well be that self-confidence is more important than being articulate ("We don't want to criticize him."). Perhaps it is. But the consequences of one's values manifest themselves every time a value-based decision is made.

Nevertheless, we do need to learn to make value-based judgments. Doing this requires understanding what our values are. Confronting a person with her own value system (one that she has unconsciously adopted) can help her think things out, but change is never easy.

ANALYTIC PROCESSES

1. Diagnosis: Making a diagnosis of a complex situation by identifying relevant factors and seeking causal explanations

Diagnosis is a very important skill and one that needs to be learned both in principle and separately for each domain of knowledge. Diagnosis of heart disease isn't a different process in principle from diagnosis of a faulty spark plug in a car engine. Nevertheless, one wants a specialist to do the diagnosis in each case. Why is this? Diagnosis is a matter of both reasoning from evidence and understanding what to look for to gather evidence. Given all the evidence, it is easy to make a diagnosis in an area of knowledge you don't know very well. So, the gathering of the evidence is the most important part. Crime analysts and gardeners both do diagnosis. They both reason from evidence. What separates them is knowing what constitutes important evidence and what does not. Here again, this comes from experienced cases.

Analytic processes involve attention to details that enable the forming of hypotheses that can be tested by a variety of methods. These three pieces, determining evidence, forming hypotheses, and testing hypotheses, are what is commonly referred to as the scientific method. When science is taught, it often dwells on the facts of science rather than the process. Diagnosis is about the process. But the process is not of much use without domain knowledge. Domain knowledge is often about causality, although that knowledge of causality may be subconscious. Experts know what causes an engine to misfire so they know where to look to find a faulty part. Experts also know that an engine is misfiring in the first place. What causes what is the real issue in the comprehension of any given domain.

We learn to do diagnosis, and to understand what causes what, consciously. This is knowledge that can be taught to us by experts, but it needs to be taught as part of the process of diagnosis. If you have a goal (understanding what is broken or has gone awry is a very typical goal), then it is much easier to acquire information that helps in the pursuit of that goal than it is to acquire that same information without that goal. To learn diagnosis, one must practice more and more complex cases in one area of knowledge.

2. Planning: Learning to plan; needs analysis; conscious and subconscious understanding of what goals are satisfied by what plans; use of conscious case-based planning

People plan constantly. Often their plans aren't very complicated. Let's have lunch is a plan, after all. Sometimes they make much more complex plans. A football coach makes plans to fool the defense. They are called plays. A general makes battlefield plans. A businessperson writes business plans. An architect draws up architectural plans. All these more complex plans have a lot in common with the let's have lunch plan. Namely, they have been used before or something quite similar has been used before. People rarely make plans from scratch. When they do, they find the process very difficult and often make many errors.

Learning to plan, therefore, has two components: being able to create a plan from scratch (which almost never actually happens) and being able to modify an existing plan for new purposes. The first one is important to learn how to do, but it is the latter ability that makes one proficient at planning. Planning from first principles is actually quite difficult. Normally people just modify an old plan. Last week we had steak; this week let's try lamb chops. This doesn't sound like rocket science and it isn't. Computer programmers write new programs by modifying old programs. Lawyers write contacts by modifying old contracts. Doctors plan procedures by thinking about past procedures. In each case, people try to improve on prior plans by remembering where these plans went wrong and then thinking about how to improve them. Acquiring a case base of plans is critical. One can modify plans from one domain of knowledge to use in another but this is not easy and requires a level of abstraction that is very important to learn. Most creative thinking depends on this ability to abstract plans from one field of knowledge to another. We learn to do this by practicing it. Teachers can help people see correspondences across domains. Abstraction of this sort is what creative people do best.

3. Causation: Detecting what has caused a sequence of events to occur by relying on a case base of previous knowledge of similar situations (case-based reasoning)

All fields of knowledge study causation: biology, physics, history, economics—they are all about what causes what. The fact that this is an object of study by academics tells us right away that it is not easy and no one knows for sure all of the causes and effects that there are in the world.

Because of this, acquiring a set of known causes and effects tends to make one an expert. A plumber knows what causes sinks to stop up and knows where to look for the culprit. A mechanic knows what causes gas lines to leak and knows where to look. A detective knows what causes people to kill and knows where to start when solving a murder case. Causal knowledge is knowledge fixed to a domain of inquiry. Experts have extensive case bases. Case bases are acquired by starting on easy cases and graduating to more complex ones. It is important to discuss with others the cases one works on because this makes one better at indexing them in one's mind, enabling one to find them later as needed.

4. Judgment: Making an objective judgment

There are two forms of this, both involving decisions based on data. The first is deciding whether you prefer Baskin Robbins or Ben and Jerry's. There is no right answer. We make judgments and then record them for use later. We find ways to express our judgments (Ben and Jerry's is too sweet, for example). We learn what we like by trying things out. A wine expert learns about wine by drinking it and recording what he thinks so he can compare his thoughts about one wine to those about a different wine later on.

The second form is reasoning based on evidence. A jury does this but it doesn't learn much from it. Judges, however, learn in this way, as do psychiatrists and businesspeople. They collect evidence, they form a judgment, and later they may get to see whether their judgment is correct. When asked, they can tell you clear reasons (typically post hoc justifications) as to why they decided the way they did. The wine expert can say reasons as well, but the evidence for taste is not really all that objective. (Of course, the evidence may be found after the judgment is made. People are not always entirely rational.)

To learn to make objective judgments, one needs constant feedback either from a teacher or from a colleague or from reality. One needs to think about what was decided and why. People who are good at this are good at it because they have analyzed their successes and failures and they can articulate their reasoning. Learning requires repeated practice.

SOCIAL PROCESSES

1. Influence: Understanding how others respond to your requests and recognizing consciously and unconsciously how to improve the process

Human interaction is one of the most important skills of all. We regularly interact with family, friends, colleagues, bosses, romantic interests, professors, service personnel, and strangers. Communicating effectively is very important to any success we might want to have in any area of life. But, we do not know why we say what we say, nor do we really understand how we are being perceived by others. We just talk and listen and go on our way. Some people are loved by everyone and others are despised. It is wrong to assume that we know what image we project or that we are easily capable of altering the way we behave so that we will be perceived differently.

How do we learn to become conscious of inherently unconscious behavior? One can learn to behave differently if one becomes consciously aware of the mistakes one is making. Watching others, watching oneself, thinking about how to improve—all this helps one make subconscious behavior into conscious behavior.

We unintentionally return to standard ways of acting in various situations. A wallflower at a party doesn't decide to be a wallflower—it is simply behavior she is comfortable with. If no one is harmed by these subconscious choices, then there is no need to fix anything. But often we might behave differently in how we treat others, if we realized what we were doing. Getting along with people is a very big part of life. Each of us has our own distinct personality, and often it doesn't match with our own ambitions and desires. To change our behavior, we need to practice new behaviors that become as natural to us as our old behaviors. The only way to do this is to do it. People can help point out what you are doing that isn't helpful to your needs but that does not mean you can easily change. If you want to change, you need to try new behaviors and practice them. This can be coached. Practicing new behaviors and being critiqued can help greatly. Written communication is handled the same way.

2. Teamwork: Learning how to achieve goals by using a team, consciously allocating roles, managing inputs from others, coordinating actors, and handling conflicts

It is the rare individual who works all alone. Most people need to work with others. Children are not naturally good at this and are taught to "share." Then they sometimes do what is called "parallel play" where they play near one another doing different things. Getting kids to cooperate to do something together is not easy. Usually one wants to dominate the others. There is nothing wrong with this per se. People are who they are and they need to assume roles in any team that are consonant with their personalities. One person plays quarterback and another blocks. People do not have to do the same thing in order to work together. But they do need to get along and function as a team. This is no more true of sports than it is of the workplace. People learn to work in teams by working in teams and receiving helpful advice when a team is dysfunctional. Football coaches explicitly teach this. More formal learning situations (like school) often don't, which is unfortunate. It really isn't possible to get along in the real world unless you can assume various roles in a team that fit with who you are.

3. Negotiation: Making a deal; negotiation/contracts

Contracts, formal and informal, are the basis of how we function. We reach agreements in business, in marriage, in friendship, in a store, and at school. Parties to those agreements have the right to complain if obligations are not met. Learning to make a contract, legal or not, is a big part of being a rational actor. To make a contract one must negotiate it. Negotiation often is seen as something only politicians and high-powered business leaders do. But, actually, we negotiate with waitresses for good service, and we negotiate with our children when we give them an allowance. Learning how to negotiate can be done only by trying and learning from failures. The techniques tend to be context-independent, but there is, of course, special knowledge about real estate and politics (for example, the relevant laws) that makes one a better negotiator in each situation. Again, practice with coaching is the ideal.

4. Describing: Creating and using conscious descriptions of situations to identify faults to be fixed

When problems exist in any situation, we need to be able to describe and analyze them. We need to be able to describe them in order to get help from people who may know more about the situation than we do. We need to learn to focus on the critical issues. In order to do this, we need also to be able to analyze these situations to see what was supposed to happen and why it isn't happening. Consultants who try to fix failing businesses do this sort of thing all the time, as do doctors when consulting on difficult cases. Creating a careful description of a situation is a skill that can be learned only through practice. This sometimes is described as learning an elevator speech to tell someone succinctly what you are doing. This ability is a very important part of understanding and helping others understand.

Now let's see what we have. First let's list again the types of cognitive processes that underlie learning:

Conceptual processes

1. Prediction
2. Judgment
3. Experimentation
4. Evaluation

Analytic processes

1. Diagnosis
2. Planning
3. Causation
4. Judgment

Social processes

1. Influence
2. Teamwork
3. Negotiation
4. Describing

What kind of stuff is this? I said above that these are cognitive processes. So let's look at them from that perspective. Let's start with the analytic processes.

What does it mean to say that diagnosis is a cognitive process? It means that there are steps and these steps are based in thought rather than in action. The first step may be to gather evidence, for example. While this seems like a physical act, and often it is, it is actually a mental act. Evidence can be gathered by asking questions, by looking carefully at a scene, by listening to sounds, or by taking blood tests. There are many ways to gather evidence, and typically the physical manifestations of evidence gathering bear no real relationship to one another. Evidence gathering is a mental act, although physical actions may be involved. It is a mental act that is part of a set of complex mental processes that, of course, include reasoning about the evidence, checking the validity of the evidence, comparing known information with previous cases that are similar, and so on. Diagnosis is a complex mental process. Teaching diagnosis matters because getting good at diagnosis can make you a good mother, a good teacher, a good detective, a good nearly anything you can think of. The process of diagnosis is constant in our mental lives.

Are all 12 of the processes listed above like this? Clearly the other analytic processes are very similar. Planning is a mental activity that one gets better at by doing it. Whether you are planning a party or planning a career, the process involves thinking about steps and imagining consequences to those steps. The more you plan, the better you get at it. We do planning every day. It matters a great deal and the better you are at it, the easier your life will go. The same is true of the third mental process: analysis of causation. Knowing why something happened allows us to not do it again—if we didn't like the end result—or to try to do it again, if we did, and everything in between. Determining causation is a mental process that is very similar to diagnosis, of course.

So these three are all cognitive processes and they require constant practice. Getting better at them throughout one's life is very important. I define learning as improvement in one's cognitive processes. Lifetime learning does not mean the continual acquisition of knowledge so much as it means the improvement in one's ability to do these processes by means of the acquisition and analysis of experiences to draw on.

CHAPTER 5

Real-Life Learning Projects Considered

I learned more about the economy from one South Dakota dust storm than I did in all my years of college.
—Hubert H. Humphrey

These days everyone has ideas about ways to improve student learning. These range from having kids stretch between classes, to listening to Mozart, to eating right. Of course, those things won't harm you, but they really have nothing to do with learning. They are about getting students to concentrate on material that doesn't interest them much. Presumably, a tedious task is made better by these kinds of things. An interesting task does not need that kind of enhancement. It should be interesting in and of itself.

In the summer of 2008, I met a most unusual man. He recently had retired from being the CEO of Epson Europe. Some years earlier, his close friend, who was director general of a college, got sick and died. His dying wish was that his friend, the Epson CEO, would succeed him and become president of the business school of the college. And so it happened that a professional from the business world found himself in charge of the Business Engineering School at La Salle University in Barcelona, Spain. During his years at Epson he had hired many graduates from that college and others, and believed that the training they received there was highly theoretical, not practical enough or oriented to the real world of business. It was clear to him that students needed a different kind of training in order to prepare them for professional life. He began to talk to the faculty about teaching different kinds of courses, ones that were less theoretical and more related to what people actually do in business. The faculty objected. Shocker.

A provost friend of mine once said that with faculty, everything is a la carte. What he meant was that professors never feel that they have to follow the wishes of the administration. They consider themselves free agents. This former CEO, coming from a business where there really is someone in charge, didn't know what to do. He talked to people who talked to people and eventually he found me.

As a professor for 30 some odd years, I developed a healthy disrespect for professors as a group. They tend to lobby for keeping their lives easy and that means, among other things, making sure they don't have to teach too much or teach in a way that makes them have to work too hard. Professors always have something more important to do than teach. I am not criticizing here. I would have been the first to whine and wail if anyone had made me teach more than one course every other quarter. I considered myself a researcher, also a graduate seminar teacher, but classes with lots of students wanting to hear a lecture? Ugh.

The college president and I had dinner and discussed what we could do together. I said we could build any program he wanted online as long as we didn't need the approval of faculty to do it and we had good experts available. He said he was the expert and we needed the approval of no one. I said it would be expensive and he said, *God will provide.* (Did I mention this school is run by the Christian Brothers?)

Two months later I found myself in front of 25 faculty in Barcelona as I interviewed the president about what someone would have to know how to do in order to make them into someone whom he would hire. He gave me a list. The faculty got to comment, but that was about it. It was clear who was in charge.

So, we built a story-centered curriculum meant to teach practical business by creating simulated experiences. The idea is to deliver it online around the world, using mentors who speak the students' language. (The website is in English). No classes. No lectures. No tests. Graduates get an MBA degree but this curriculum doesn't have that much in common with traditional MBA programs. The idea is to help people launch their own business or go to work.

Students are part of teams that work to create deliverables within a story about a situation that demands some work on their part. They consult with their team members and use extensive background and step-by-step help that has been created as part of the website. Mentors are available to answer questions and to evaluate the final work product. The projects are large enough that students need to divide up the work and consult with one another on how to proceed. Eventually they create a deliverable and either continue to work on improving it after receiving feedback from the mentor or move on to the next subtask in the story.

I will describe briefly the stories that the students work within (they each last anywhere from 6 to 9 weeks). Then I want to consider what these courses are really teaching from the perspective of the framework of cognitive processes that I described in Chapter 4.

COURSE 1: "CASH CRISIS"—
ANALYZE AND SOLVE FINANCIAL BUSINESS PROBLEMS

The story for this course is that a family that owns a winery business hires a consulting firm to help determine why the bank denied the renewal of a loan. The students, working in the role of assistant consultants, first conduct financial analyses to determine problems within the business. Next, they conduct a root cause analysis to determine the underlying causes of the problems affecting the business. Students then develop solutions to address the problems and write a report outlining the solutions, including 5-year financial projections.

COURSE 2: "GOING ONLINE"—
TAKE A SMALL BUSINESS ONLINE

Students are contacted by an investor who is interested in starting an online business selling gift baskets. She wants the students to help her plan what the business will sell in the gift baskets and to design the user interface for the website. She is leaving it up to the students to determine what sort of gift basket business they want to design. Her immediate concern is seeing what the site would look like, and how it would function, to make sure she will have a good design to impress prospective buyers.

Students begin by interviewing prospective customers and seeing how they typically buy such items online, to learn from their usage patterns and to determine common breakdowns in the usual process. Next, students produce expected user scenarios for the "personas" they identify as being prospective users of the site. They then define functional and nonfunctional requirements for the site they must design. They design the information architecture, including content, sitemap, wireframes, and low-fi prototypes, after which they test their prototypes on prospective users. The final step in the process is a review of proposals from a set of vendors who could build the site the students designed.

COURSE 3: MARKETING—LAUNCHING A NEW PRODUCT

In this story, the students belong to a product-launching team. The goal is to launch a new social network for amateur performers, iSing. com. Students decide which role they want to play, product marketing or marketing communication, and working together in teams of four, they prepare the launching plan for this product. Among the activities they perform are preparing job descriptions for both roles, preparing a position strategy statement and a message architecture, preparing a preliminary market segmentation for the product, preparing demographics and psychographics of the target groups, launching a kick-off meeting for the project, and preparing a launching program, including the following subtasks: total product requirements, barriers to customer adoption, competitive analysis, market/customer research, hiring a research firm, market leverage model, communication plan, web tools, branding, market research, and hiring a PR firm. Finally, students prepare a complete budget and defend the plan and the budget in front of the top management of the company.

COURSE 4: RE-ENGINEER A SUPPLY CHAIN

Students now play the role of junior executive in the supply chain management department of RightByte technologies. They receive a report from the CEO describing the current processes and the main problems identified. With this information, students are requested to find out the root causes of the problems and come up with a suggested course of action to solve them. They have to take into account the following design principles for the new solution: customer service impact, impact on cost savings, and ease of implementation.

From this point on, the teams analyze each piece of the supply chain to make the deep diagnosis: demand/supply planning, transportation, warehouse management, sales order management, and central order fulfillment. Once the diagnosis and requirements are well established, the teams develop a suggested solution. Finally, top management requires the team to prepare a change management evaluation to see whether the company is prepared to undertake such a complex project.

COURSE 5: INVESTMENT READINESS— HELP A SMALL TECHNOLOGICAL COMPANY TO SUCCESSFULLY RAISE FUNDS FOR AN INTERNATIONAL EXPANSION IN A SECOND ROUND

Next.TV is a small company that has been very successful in the local market. It has developed a software package to automate an editorial department of a TV channel. Most of the main domestic channels have already implemented the package and the company wants to go international. Students are hired as expert consultants to prepare the company for this second round of financing and to present the project to Venture Capital firms. Students now do several tasks that they have already done in the previous modules, plus some new tasks, but they do them now in an integrated manner and with much less time to finish them. Task to perform are: analyze starting point (P&L and balance sheet), enhance the product value proposition, prepare a sales plan, perform a management audit, prepare the internalization plan, prepare financial planning, write the business plan, identify potential VC firms to present to, analyze offerings, and negotiate a term sheet.

COURSE 6: ETHICAL AND LEGAL ISSUES IN CORPORATE GOVERNANCE

This course involves reading and discussing a specially written novel. The intent of the novel is to inspire readers to wrestle with the problems of the characters, who are involved in complex ethical and moral decisions within the pharmaceutical industry. The novel serves as a starting point for the kind of active contemplation and discussion that truly make people better able to think more deeply about such issues. The students immerse themselves in the story of an international pharmaceutical company engaged in a hostile takeover of a smaller, but highly successful, competitor. Students experience the tough negotiations, the elimination of dedicated and talented individuals, and the painful shuffling of roles and responsibilities that accompany major change in a modern corporation. Students also confront the complicated (and sometimes conflicting) relationship between social responsibility, legal responsibility, and profit motive, as they witness the company's attempt to establish a new research facility in a blighted town as a consequence of the merger. As students consider each episode, they critique the actions and reactions of the central characters, advise them on next steps, and glean lessons related to negotiation, change management, legal and ethical issues in corporate governance, and working with other cultures.

STORY 7: SELLING AND IMPLEMENTING SOLUTIONS

Students begin their work as new project managers at a premier event-planning company, World Class Events. They begin by qualifying and prioritizing opportunities to propose work to prospective clients, pitching to senior management which of the proposals should receive the greatest budget, based on potential profitability, likelihood of winning, and other relevant considerations. They create a project scope document for the sales effort, first planning and attending a simulated meeting with event-planning experts to determine a vision for the event, including risks and open questions for the client. They then engage in a role-play call with the client, introducing World Class Events and clarifying the project vision.

Of course, the intent of this curriculum is to prepare students to go out into the business world. So, there is a natural subject orientation. The subject is business. But after we acknowledge that, everything else is different. The curriculum was designed with the 12 cognitive processes in mind. Let's see how that was accomplished.

The real issue in learning in any arena of knowledge is getting better at the cognitive processes that underlie that knowledge. The processes involved in learning have been with us as long as there have been humans. School, and subject-based education, is a more recent invention. To understand how human learning works, we need to think more deeply about how we can teach these processes.

So, we might ask, Where do the 12 cognitive processes get taught in this MBA program?

First let's list the cognitive processes again:

Conceptual processes

1. Prediction
2. Judgment
3. Experimentation
4. Evaluation

Analytic processes

1. Diagnosis
2. Planning
3. Causation
4. Judgment

Social processes

1. Influence
2. Teamwork
3. Negotiation
4. Describing

Now let's consider them one at a time.

Where is prediction taught in our MBA program?

In course 1 (cash crisis), students have to create a financial plan. Any planning document is a serious attempt at prediction. Prediction is covered in a different way in course 2. In that course, students need to predict how users will behave on a website. In course 3, students need to predict the effects of a marketing campaign and predict what will work and what will not work in a product launch. In course 4, students need to predict how changes they make in the supply chain will improve the process. In course 5, students are developing a business model, which is in itself a prediction that certain decisions and behaviors will make money. In course 6, students must predict the effects of various changes in an organization and must predict the behavior of the people with whom they will negotiate. In course 7, students predict which sales pitches will work as well as predicting various costs and benefits associated with their product.

In fact, it seems obvious that *prediction* is at the very heart of this MBA program. But so are all the other cognitive processes. Students are always working in *teams* and are always trying to *influence* their peers, their superiors, their customers, and so on. They are in constant *negotiations* and they are creating all kinds of *plans*—financial plans, marketing plans, and business plans. They are constantly *diagnosing* problems in the various stories and constantly creating documents as work products (*describing*). They must determine the *cause* of various problems in each story and *evaluate* solutions to those problems. They make *judgments* about what to do, and what is working and what isn't, in each story and they create *models* of proposed solutions. Each new solution they propose is, in effect, an *experiment,* and they must evaluate the results of each experiment as they proceed.

Now let's reconsider what it means to teach and what is important to teach within the context of a good curriculum. One might have expected, given that there are 12 cognitive processes that must be learned, that each project in the curriculum would be put clearly into one of the categories. The schooling mentality naturally leads to the idea that if diagnosis is important, then we should offer a course in diagnosis. But you can't diagnose randomly and you can't teach students to do diagnosis in the absence of an acknowledgment of their real interest and goals independent of a context. While diagnosis is fundamentally the same process whether you are plumber, a doctor, or a businessperson, there is also much to learn about the context of the diagnosis, and real students with real goals will fall asleep while hearing about diagnosis in one context, whereas they will perk up while actually doing diagnosis in a context they find fascinating.

We have designed this curriculum to teach the 12 cognitive processes within the context that was decided upon by the students. No one is forced to take an MBA program. The students are those who want to run their own business or work within the context of a large business. It is the job of the curriculum designer (and the teacher), therefore, to teach them how to think well within that context.

Now I am not saying that this is not done (or at least cannot be done) within traditional schooling. Sometimes it is. A good history teacher does in fact teach about diagnosis and causation and planning. One can think about the Battle of Waterloo and learn a great deal about planning, and influence, and causation, and teamwork.

But while this could be true of a good history course, it often is in no way actually the case. If history courses were designed to teach students to think within the context of history, they would be much more important than they now are. As long as we think that history is about getting the facts about who signed what declaration when, we are missing the forest for the trees from a teaching point of view.

Now, of course, some subjects lend themselves very easily to emphasis of the 12 cognitive processes. Science courses could, for example, be entirely about experimentation or diagnosis or causation, and they would be very useful if they were. But instead we encourage learning the facts about who did what experiment and we teach formulas to be memorized and we teach about equations. Experimentation is indeed a very exciting subject. (Ask any 2-year-old who experiments with what best goes in his mouth on a daily basis.) But schooling manages to make it a very dull subject by teaching who did what experiment when.

One reason that we have managed to create dullness out of material that can be inherently interesting is the absurd emphasis on testing that has dominated the world of education in the past years. Below are three questions (quite typical ones) from an AP psychology exam.

Ivan P. Pavlov is famous for his research on

(A) teaching machines.
(B) perceptual learning.
(C) forward conditioning.
(D) classical conditioning.
(E) backward conditioning.

A stimulus that elicits a response before the experimental manipulation is a (an)

(A) response stimulus (RS).
(B) unconditioned stimulus (UCS).
(C) generalized stimulus (GS).
(D) conditioned stimulus (CS).
(E) specific stimulus (SS).

Erikson proposed that trust or mistrust develops during the

(A) muscular-anal stage.
(B) locomotor-genital stage.
(C) latency stage.
(D) oral-sensory stage.
(E) maturity stage.

Psychology is all about experimentation, but the questions here are about facts about previous experiments, which is very different from learning to design and perform an experiment about something that personally interests you. Psychology teachers cannot teach students how to create a hypothesis and experiment to find out whether it is true, unless they go around the existing curriculum. Since teachers are judged by their students' results on AP tests, this is hardly likely.

Another problem here is that only some of the 12 cognitive processes are conscious. Others are hidden from our conscious minds. If school were to actively try to teach diagnosis, for example, soon enough there would be the 18 principles of diagnosis or a test about who said what about diagnosis. There probably wouldn't be much actual diagnosis unless something drastically changed our conception of what schooling should look like.

The major problem with how we think about teaching is our conception of what it means to teach, as well as our conception of what it means to learn. In school we "know" that one has to learn math and science and literature. I am asserting here that it is that notion, that there are these specific subjects to teach, that has ruined our schools.

There are abilities to teach, not subjects.

Academics designed the school system. To them, it seemed natural that the subjects that they were experts on should be taught in high school. Such a simple thought has created a major problem.[1] Education ought not be subject-based but, in a sense, we can't help but think of it that way because we all went to schools that were subject-based. Even corporate training, which need not be subject-based, tends to be viewed in that way as well, simply because that is the way we have always looked at education owing to our own experiences in school.

Once you set up the learning question in terms of subjects that need to be taught, it is very tempting to use the old tried and true, *Why don't we just tell them the facts and any underlying theories?* The knowledge metaphor, the one that says that teachers know some stuff that students don't, naturally leads teachers to tell students what they know.

Now let's consider corporate training.

The companies that contract with my company[2] to build courses know that we will not use the *learning by telling* method. Presumably they are frustrated with the results that the telling method has produced in courses that have been built for them by others. (In fact, they refer to it as "death by PowerPoint.") This is why they come to us. Still they can't help but ask the same subject-based question. How could they not? It is all they know. They went to school. They see the world in the way that school taught them to see it.

They don't ask the questions they should ask because they can't. We need to transform badly formed educational questions into properly formed ones. We need to transform subject-based questions into cognitive process-based questions. This means changing statements about the need to manage client relationships into statements about cognition, and statements about product launch into ones about cognition, and so on. What does it mean to make such transformations? It means asking what one does when one manages client relationships or when one launches a product. This is, of course, exactly what we ask clients in our first meeting with them. For example, we ask: *What does one do when one launches a product?*

What I plan to do here is reveal what we do next, namely, the *subject to cognitive ability transformation process*. We must do the transformation properly and then make clear what one does in course design after one has figured out what really needs to be taught.

Let's start simple. Let's imagine we want to train insurance adjusters to decide what compensation a policy owner is entitled to after a hurricane hits his property. (Yes, I do live in Florida, but I can't say I care much about this process personally.) I found this on the Internet covering this subject:

Catastrophe Adjusting Refresher

Course Description: This is a course package comprised of three courses plus a bonus section and downloadable documents.

One of the three courses is this:

Catastrophe Adjusting Skills and Techniques

Course Description: This is a course package comprised of seven courses plus two bonus sections and a number of downloadable documents.

This online class is for individuals who are new to adjusting catastrophes, such as hurricanes, windstorms, and tornadoes. The course is broken down into two key sections: "Getting Prepared for Adjusting" and "The Actual Adjusting Process." The first section includes a number of course components and background knowledge that can be done in preparation for any catastrophe. The second part of the class takes you through all the steps and processes required for adjusting residential properties. This online package includes everything listed under course topics.

Course Topics:

- Insurance Basics
- Tools of the Trade
- Working with Digital Photos
- Residential Construction Basics
- Claim File Components
- Homeowners Policy Interpretation
- Property Adjusting 101
- Getting organized
- Claim reporting

Course Length: 8 hours

Audience: Property adjusters who are new to processing and adjusting catastrophe claims and need the knowledge and skills required to be successful on the job.

One thing that jumps out here is the time. In 8 hours, the above topics will all be covered.

Wow! Assuming an hour for each subject, this means you can learn insurance basics, or residential construction basics, in an hour if you take this course. What this means in practice, I assume, is that there will be some text to read and some questions to answer to make sure that you have read the text. Personally, I doubt that one could learn much about any of these subjects by oneself in 8 hours (or even 8 days.) Clearly, they are teaching vocabulary and a few facts. Most of it will be forgotten.

Now suppose the insurance industry had come to me and asked my company to build a course that covered these topics. What would I say? (Apart from: *Are you nuts?—not in 8 hours.*)

I would start by asking what is hard about insurance adjusting. At the same time, I would have already assumed that this was basically a diagnosis task.

Diagnosis is a complex cognitive process that has three important parts. The most important part is the end result. All successful diagnoses result in an answer (cancer, stopped up sewer line, misfiring spark plug, paranoia, etc.). These results are taken from a list of acceptable answers and typically are not in any way inventive. The second part is the case. A prototypical case for all possible results typically is compared with the current case. A match determines the result. The third part is the evidence. To construct a case, one must gather evidence. When more than one prototypical case matches the situation, more evidence needs to be gathered in order to differentiate the cases that might match. Doctors call this differential diagnosis.

How does one learn to do diagnosis? One must know the prototypical case, which often takes years for one to acquire naturally through experience. One must know how to gather evidence, and what constitutes evidence, and one must know the possible set of results. All of this takes a long time to learn. But the process itself is very much the same no matter what you are diagnosing. So, one question we would ask was whether the students in the course had any experience diagnosing anything. It is easier to teach diagnosis to people who have done it before even if the subject matter is different this time. Another question we would ask is how much the students knew about the basics of the subject matter since it is easier to teach diagnosis to those who already know the subject matter.

So when I ask what is hard about insurance adjusting, I have a good idea of what the answer may be. It is probably in one of these three things. Is it difficult to learn all the kinds of cases that there are and what differentiates one from another? This depends on how many types of cases there are. Is it hard to gather evidence properly? Probably. It usually is. Is it hard to know all the possible results? It might not be. It might be hard to decide on a result, however, since the result is usually to pay some amount of money, so how much money would be the key question. All this takes practice, so what we really need to know is where the main areas of practice should be.

So now we have a real question to ask:

Q1: How can we practice gathering evidence, learning about prototypical cases, and knowing how to determine the correct final result in insurance adjusting?

Notice that this is a very different question from asking what an insurance adjuster knows and then asking how to tell students what they should know.

Making the transformation from the list of knowledge given above by the online course offerers into Q1 is the real issue in transforming subject-based education into cognitive process-based education.

Let's discuss a different type of example. My company was invited into a technical college in Peru to discuss how to teach accounting. *Why would you want to teach accounting?* I asked. Because the students need to know it, I was told. *Why?* I said. Because they need it in their work. So I changed the subject. I asked, *What work do most people do when they graduate from your school?*

It turns out most of their graduates ran fast-food restaurants. *Then why do they need to learn accounting?* They need it in order to run a restaurant. I am sure there is some accounting done as part of running a restaurant, but surely not every part of accounting is needed. And, I asked, *Do you actually teach how to run a restaurant?*

Of course they didn't. Why not? Because accounting is an academic subject and managing fast-food employees and ordering meat are not. They hire an accounting professor, and he knows accounting and knows nothing about running a restaurant. Even a practical technical school gets caught up in subject-based education in part because it hires graduates from that system who know only what they themselves were taught.

What are the cognitive processes involved in running a fast-food restaurant? Let's see which are relevant.

Conceptual processes

1. Prediction   YES
2. Modeling   YES
3. Experimentation   YES
4. Evaluation   YES

Analytic processes

1. Diagnosis   YES
2. Planning   YES
3. Causation   YES
4. Judgment   YES

Social processes

1. Influence   YES
2. Teamwork   YES
3. Negotiation   YES
4. Describing   YES

Hmm. All of them. How can this be?

Managing a business, any business, requires one to influence employees, negotiate with suppliers, plan future moves, determine what isn't working, teach employees how to work together, make judgments about people and processes, and so on.

All this should give a hint about how to approach a business that wants to teach its employees to do their jobs properly. One must teach each of the 12 processes, but they need to be taught in the actual context of what people will do when they graduate. This does not mean that for every problem there are 12 courses that need to be created.

While you might need to predict an employee's behavior, this does not mean there should be a prediction course. This is not a problem because there never is such a course. A businessperson has to make judgments, and determine causes of problems, and so on, so maybe we should have courses in each of those processes. But this makes no sense.

We must teach people to deal with the real-life issues that arise in any situation they are preparing to work in. In other words, the designer of a course on how to manage a restaurant must focus on the typical goal conflict situations that a new manager would have to confront. The course designer must create a fictional situation where it is necessary to convince an employee to do something or to find out why something that was asked of an employee did not happen.

The magic word is *scenario*. Scenarios are like plays. Things happen and you have to deal with them. A well-written scenario makes sure that all of the processes that could be at all relevant to what you want to teach, occur in this new context. In a reasonable education system, students would have been practicing all of these processes all of their lives. But we do not have a reasonable education system. We have one based in subjects. So our cognitive processes are not rehearsed over time in different contexts by constant practice. Instead we learn knowledge about subjects.

To remedy this, a course designer (and a teacher if the teacher has that freedom) must make sure that as many of the cognitive processes as are relevant to a situation naturally occur within the scenario being constructed to simulate what will happen in real life later on. Not every situation requires diagnosis, but many do. Not every situation has a goal conflict or forces one to make predictions or plans, but many do. If what needs to be taught naturally lends itself to working on any of the 12 cognitive processes, then the training being built must concentrate on that. If there could be diagnosis, then there should be training in diagnosis in that context, and that training must supersede the garnering of facts.

Schools are tough to change. We are trying, but the subject-based educators have a few hundred years head start. However, in designing new training, it is quite possible to reorient subject-based courses and turn them into cognitive process-based courses that are much more satisfying to both the teacher and the student.

CHAPTER 6

A Socratic Dialogue

Sit down before fact as a little child, be prepared to give up every conceived notion, follow humbly wherever and whatever abysses nature leads, or you will learn nothing.

—Thomas Huxley

Slave Boy: So it really doesn't matter how you classify a teaching/learning problem because there are many methods that could apply, correct?

Socrates: And what follows from this?

Slave Boy: That it is not the classification that matters but the methods entailed in that classification.

Socrates: And what do all these methods have in common?

Slave Boy: They all involve practice.

Socrates: And what else?

Slave Boy: Real experience.

Socrates: And how is experience stored?

Slave Boy: Through cases.

Socrates: Expressed how?

Slave Boy: As stories.

Socrates: So what follows from all this?

Slave Boy: That the methodology entailed in each classification of learning types is not the real issue.

Socrates: And what is the real issue?

Slave Boy: Practice.

Socrates: And?

Slave Boy: Dialogue.

Socrates: Why dialogue?

Slave Boy: Because it is through dialogue that stories are solidified and indexed.

Socrates: So the classification of learning types doesn't really matter then, does it?

Slave Boy: Oh no, dear teacher, I beg to differ. The classification helps
    us think about the real issues in education.
Socrates: Indeed.

CHAPTER 7

Knowledge-Based Education vs. Process-Based Education

Diagnosis is not the end, but the beginning of practice.
—Martin H. Fischer

In our society we have set up schools to teach knowledge. We concern ourselves with what facts children know, we test to make sure they know them, and then we complain that the schools are failing when they don't. This idea is so ingrained in our way of looking at schooling that when people like me complain about it, we are seen as people who are rambling around muttering to ourselves.

There are so many people having anxiety attacks about what kids know, it seems one can find an article about it in every news segment on education.

I happened on an article in *Huffington Post* written by someone named Schweitzer who is listed as "having served at the White House during the Clinton Administration as Assistant Director for International Affairs in the Office of Science and Technology Policy." Here is a piece of what he said:

> The health care debate cannot be understood in historic context because many Americans have never heard of Thomas Jefferson. Extrapolating from state surveys, only 14% of American high school students can name who wrote the Declaration of Independence. Nearly 75% do not know that George Washington was our first president. . . . We can say that our educational system has failed when the vast majority of American students do not know enough to pass an exam to qualify as American citizens.

This is an astonishing statement.

Why do we have such a failed system? Could it be the policies of presidents like Clinton, who pursued a policy of never offending the teachers unions by doing anything threatening to them, like changing the curriculum?

Or, could it be that people such as this writer define education in terms of random facts they wished everyone knew? The problem is not that people don't know who Thomas Jefferson was. If citizens knew who he was, would that mean that they could think clearly and not be influenced by all the special interests who were trying to tell them what to think? If they knew who George Washington was, what exactly would they know about him? That he could never tell a lie? This is obviously untrue, and many have written about what a good liar he actually was. That he was a brilliant general? There is lots of evidence against that. That he owned 300 slaves? This is not usually mentioned. That he married a rich woman probably so he could get her land? Historians discuss this. Schools never do. Nevertheless, people are upset because our students don't know our national myths and some random facts.

The real issue in the healthcare debate is that the general public can't think clearly. That would have a simple explanation. The schools don't even try to teach people to think clearly.

I mentioned President Clinton above, but really all U.S. presidents are culpable. It may not be their fault. Certainly they are given terrible information.

Lamar Alexander, former Secretary of Education (under George H.W. Bush) was speaking in the U.S. Senate recently on restoring teaching history to its "rightful place" and making sure that history was part of the NCLB act. Here is a quote from him from 2006:

> Just one example of how far we are from helping our children learn what they need to know. The fourth grade national report card test asked students to identify the following passage, "We hold these truths to be self-evident that all men are created equal, that they are endowed by their Creator with certain unalienable rights, that among these are Life, Liberty, and the Pursuit of Happiness." Students were given four choices: Constitution, Mayflower Compact, Declaration of Independence, and Articles of Confederation. Less than

half the students answered correctly that that came from the Declaration of Independence. Another question said, "Imagine that you landed in Philadelphia in the summer of 1776. Describe an important event that is happening there." Nearly half the students couldn't answer the question correctly that the Declaration of Independence was being signed.

Politicians never seem to get it about education. What history do students "need to know"? None, actually, unless they plan on being historians, or maybe senators. Now I realize this is a radical point of view, but history is not something anyone needs to know.

Why not?

Because knowing what happened in Philadelphia in 1776 does not in fact make you a better citizen, no matter what Alexander says. Random historical "facts" do not make one a critical thinker about history nor do they promote clear thinking about current political issues. Such "facts" are almost always used by politicians to justify whatever it is they already believe. Understanding how human events typically flow is, in fact, quite valuable, but that has more to do with understanding human nature and prior circumstances than it does with memorizing facts that politicians deem important to know. A good citizen would be one who carefully considered the issues when voting. That would mean being able to diagnose problems and evaluate proposed solutions. But that would produce a citizenry that could ask hard questions of politicians, which is probably not what these politicians are aiming for.

In 1776 we had a bunch of politicians who, if the present set are any example, surely were voting for their own special interests. The fact that we, as a country, feel the need to make them into folk heroes does not make it one bit more likely they were any better or worse than the current people who govern us. What Alexander is really arguing for is more indoctrination—more informing students what to think instead of teaching them how to think.

It would be nice if one simply could point a finger and say it is all the politicians' fault. They really don't want people to think all that clearly. But politicians are only part of the problem.

Recently, a report was issued about the teaching of mathematics, stating:

Students who complete Algebra II are more than twice as likely to graduate from college compared to students with less mathematical preparation.[1]

The natural assumption here is that we must hurry up and teach more Algebra II, of course. Except that obviously is not what is going on; it just serves the interests of those who wrote the report to put it that way. Here is another statement from that report:

Students who depended on their native intelligence learned less than those who believed that success depended on how hard they worked.

The claim is simply this: If you work harder, you get into college. Now the question is: Why are the writers of this report claiming that the thing that students have to work harder at is Algebra II?

It is easy enough to see why this panel decided that. At stake was a $100 million federal budget request for *Math Now*, and the people who were on the panel were people who would receive that funding. University professors issue reports asking for grant money to be approved that state that the nation will not succeed without that grant money. Vested interests are nothing new. I am sometimes amazed that no one points this stuff out, however. *It is well established that everyone must know algebra.* The fact that this is well established by those who make money on the teaching of algebra is never brought up by the *New York Times*, which published a lead article on the report, or by anyone else, it seems.

My favorite part of the *Times* article was the following:

Dr. Faulkner, a former president of the University of Texas at Austin, said the panel "buys the notion from cognitive science that kids have to know the facts."

Dr. Faulkner, let me point out, is a chemist, and I am pretty sure he doesn't really know much about cognitive science. But cognitive science has been used of late to justify a great deal of what is wrong in education. E.D. Hirsch, an English professor at the University of Virginia, made a career of making lists of stuff every kid should know. When cognitive scientists trashed this work as nonsense, he cited the idea that one needs background knowledge in order to read, which is both true and a product of various works in cognitive science.

Hirsch was made to look like a fool so often that he resorted to hiring a cognitive science professor at Virginia, who has written a book justifying the same nonsense with more cognitive science facts.[2]

There is plenty of work in cognitive science that shows that background knowledge helps people interpret the world around them, and thus reading, for example, is facilitated by having knowledge about the world about which you are reading. This idea, however, does not imply that ramming facts down a kid's throat is the way for them to acquire that background knowledge. Knowledge acquisition is a natural result of engaging in cognitive processes that are being employed to satisfy a truly held goal.

If you are trying to find your way around a city, you will learn the streets of that city and develop what is called a cognitive map. If you try to memorize those same streets, it simply won't work. Real knowledge is acquired as a natural part of an employed cognitive process in service of a goal. But Hirsch and Willingham know nothing about cognitive processes. They only know, and talk about, how best to acquire more facts. Politicians listen to them and there are more tests to make sure those facts have been acquired. No one remembers Algebra II or much about the Founding Fathers because that stuff is mostly facts acquired independent of any real goals that will employ those facts. Knowledge is not the real issue in education or in mental life. The real issue is developing facility with doing various cognitive processes. Knowledge comes along for free with practice of these processes in specific domains.

There is no evidence whatsoever that accumulation of facts and background knowledge are the same thing. In fact, there is plenty of evidence to the contrary. Facts learned out of context, and apart from actual real-world experience that is repeated over and over, are not retained.

Why don't kids like school? Because we teach them knowledge that they know they won't need. How do they know this? They know that their parents don't know this stuff—that is how. Many kids don't like math much and it is clear why. They find it boring and irrelevant to anything they care about doing. If we think math is so important, then why not teach it within a meaningful context, where it actually is used? There is plenty of evidence that shows that teaching math within a real and meaningful context works a whole lot better than shoving it down their throats and following that with a multiple choice test. But for the vast majority of citizens, Algebra II is never used.

There is no evidence whatsoever that says that a nation that is trailing in math test scores will somehow trail in GDP or whatever it is we really care about. This is just plain silly, but we keep repeating the mantra that we are behind Korea in math as if it has been proven that this matters in some way. Nothing of the sort has been proven. What is true is that there are a great many vested interests that need to keep teaching math: tutoring companies, testing companies, math teachers, book publishers, and many others who make lots of money when people are scared into thinking that their kid won't get into college because he or she is bad at Algebra II. Nearly every grownup has forgotten whatever algebra he or she ever learned to pass those silly tests, so it is clear that algebra is meaningless for adult life. Any college professor who is honest will tell you that algebra almost never comes up in any college course, and when it does come up it usually needn't be there in the first place.

So, math isn't important and history isn't important. What is important?

Tests. Tests are very important. Not to me, of course, but my vote isn't being counted.

The past two presidents have been obsessed with raising test scores. I am assuming this is true because some political analysts somewhere have determined that the general public believes in the significance of raising tests scores and will vote for politicians who are able to show that they have done it. There can't be any other reason. Try taking those tests. Most of them are available online. See how well you can do at them.

But what could really be wrong with testing and emphasizing test scores?

TESTING TEACHES THAT THERE ARE RIGHT ANSWERS

The problem is that in real life, the important questions don't have answers that are clearly right or wrong. "Knowing the answer" has made school into Jeopardy. It is nice to win a game show, but important decisions are made through argumentation and force of reason—not by knowing the right answer. People who know a lot are generally quite smart. I could do well at Jeopardy as could most professors, I would think. But we are not successful intellectuals because we know a lot of facts. We know a lot of facts because we are successful intellectuals. People have got this backwards.

Consider athletes. A great baseball player and a great basketball player, it can be assumed, also will be very good at lifting weights. But they did not become good at lifting weights and then become great athletes. It was the other way around. They had a natural talent for hitting a ball or shooting baskets and then they had to get stronger in order to compete with others who had the same talents. The talent is the reason—not the weightlifting. Michael Jordan, a really great athlete, couldn't become a successful baseball player because he couldn't hit a curve ball. That talent had nothing to do with the athletic ability that made him a great basketball player. Hitting a curve ball is a different kind of talent. His weightlifting ability was the same either way. I know a lot of facts and I am talented at designing educational software. The facts I know do not help with the talent. But the more educational software I design in different domains of knowledge, the more facts I pick up.

When we look at people who are knowledgeable and confuse that with people who can think well, we totally miss the point about education. Education ought not be focused on imparting facts any more than athletic training ought to be focused on weightlifting. You learn to hit a ball by hitting one, and you learn to think clearly by thinking. Focusing on the 12 cognitive processes I have outlined, rather than focusing on fact acquisition, helps one learn to think.

TESTING TEACHES THAT SOME SUBJECTS ARE MORE IMPORTANT THAN OTHERS

The tests are small in number. If there were thousands to choose from, then perhaps people could get tested in fiber optics instead of history. But the system has determined which subjects are the most important. The system made that determination in 1892. Some things have changed in the world since then. There are a few new subjects—psychology, computers, medicine, business, and law, for example. Many new sciences and social sciences came into being after 1892. But none of those will ever make it into the sacred group of math, science, English, economics, and history because everyone seems to think that the big five were handed down on tablets to Moses.

And everyone is sure that their favorite subject is the most important one, be it history, literature, math, or science. Math and science are having a big moment as I write this. We hear that the nation does not produce enough students interested in math and science. Something must be done.

I was a math major in college. I got 98 on every math Regents test offered. (I lived in New York where testing ruled in the world in the 1950s too.) My mother always asked where the other two points went. I grew up to be a computer science professor. I am not a math phobe. But neither am I a math proponent. I have never used math in my professional life.

I always start any discussion on education by asking if the person I am talking with knows the quadratic formula. One out of one hundred knows it. (The last few times I asked, the people included the head of a major testing service, the governor of a U.S. state, various state legislators, and 200 high school principals.) Then why do we teach this obviously useless piece of information to every student in the world? Because math is important, of course.

Why?

As a person who was involved with graduate admissions for 30 years at three of the top ten universities in the country, I know what this hysteria is actually about. Nearly all applicants to graduate computer science programs (which is what I know—but it is true in most fields of engineering and science) are foreign nationals. We wonder why American kids aren't interested in these fields—which is a reasonable enough question. But then we have come up with an extraordinary answer.

What we say is that we must teach math and science better in high school when what we mean is that it would be nice to have some more American-born scientists.

Do we really believe that the reason that there are so many foreign applicants to U.S. graduate programs is that they teach math and science better in other countries? China and India provide most of the applicants. They also have most of the world's people. And many of those people will do anything to live in the United States. So they cram math down their own throats, knowing that it is a ticket to America. Very few of these applicants come from Germany, Sweden, France, or Italy. Is this because they teach math badly there or is it because those people aren't desperate to move to the United States?

U.S. students are not desperate to move to the United States, so when you suggest to them that they numb themselves with formulas and equations, they refuse to do so. The right answer would be to make math and science actually interesting, but with those awful tests as the ultimate arbiter of success, this is very difficult to do. Math and science are not important subjects. There, I said it. Start the lynching. One can live a happy life without ever having taken a physics course or knowing what a logarithm is.

But being able to reason on the basis of evidence actually is important. You cannot live well without this skill (or any of the other cognitive processes I have been writing about). Diagnosis is science as it actually is practiced by scientists. Science is not a bunch of stuff to be memorized. It is the fact-based tests that cause this problem. We don't need more math and science. We need more people who can think.

TESTING FOCUSES TEACHERS ON WINNING NOT TEACHING

Many teachers are extremely frustrated by the system they have found themselves a part of. They cannot afford to spend time teaching a student or getting a concept across if the issues being taught are not on the tests. They are judged on the basis of test scores. So any rational teacher gives up teaching and becomes a kind of test preparation coach. Testing has become a kind of contest between schools, much like football. I like football. But the football mentality that envelops our concept of schooling is a disaster.

Take a look at this excerpt of an article taken from my local paper. What our educators are worrying about is winning the game. Unfortunately, the game has nothing to do with educating students and everything to do with test scores, which are probably less valuable than football scores in predicting anything about the future of children's lives.

Martin County School District won't settle for B

July 27, 2007

STUART—The Martin County School District was just short of earning a perfect report card from the state in late June.

But the district, which earned 18 A's and one B, has a chance to earn straight A's. School officials are appealing J.D. Parker School of Science, Math & Technology's B grade. The Stuart elementary school had enough points to be considered an "A" school, but because the lowest 25 percent of the school's students didn't make learning gains, the state dropped the grade to a B.

. . . .

Martin had the second-highest percentage of A schools among the state's 67 counties. Gilchrist County had the highest percentage of A's, though the county in northeastern Florida only has four schools.

The district is also filing an appeal for Warfield Elementary in Indiantown. The school received an A, but did not make adequate yearly progress under the federal No Child Left Behind Act, state data shows.

The result of all this is that teachers are now being "held accountable" for their teaching, which is another way of saying, *Get those test scores up or else.*

The following is from an article on the front page of the *New York Times* (December 23, 2007):

Mr. Obama, for instance, in a speech last month in New Hampshire denounced the law (NCLB) as "demoralizing our teachers." But he also said it was right to hold all children to high standards. "The goals of this law were the right ones," he said.

When Mr. Edwards released an education plan earlier this year, he said the No Child law needed a "total overhaul." But he said he would continue the law's emphasis on accountability.

And at the elementary school in Waterloo, Mrs. Clinton said she would "do everything I can as senator, but if we don't get it done, then as president, to end the unfunded mandate known as No Child Left Behind."

But she, too, added: "We do need accountability."

Accountability must play well in Peoria because every politician is for it.

Accountability must mean to voters, I assume, that teachers will be measured by how well they teach their students. Political candidates, always willing to hop on an uncontroversial point of view, are all quite certain that the voters know what they are talking about. No matter how stupid NCLB is, no matter how mean spirited, no matter how awful for both teachers and students, its very horror rests on the premise that no one seems to be disputing that the federal government has the right to tell the schools what to teach and to see whether they are indeed teaching it.

How is this premise wrong?

- It assumes that all schools should teach the same subjects.
- It assumes that some subjects are more important than other subjects.
- It assumes that all important subjects can be easily tested.
- It assumes that seeing who did better than whom in school is an intrinsic part of the educational process.
- It assumes that all children have the same educational needs.

Let's take them one by one.

ALL SCHOOLS SHOULD TEACH THE SAME SUBJECTS

Why is this wrong?

First, it is wrong because subjects aren't what should be taught. But even if one follows the view presented in this book that the issue is cognitive processes and not subjects, cognitive processes need to be applied to actual domains, that are relevant to the life of the student. Kids in New York come from, and will live in, a different world than their compatriots in New Mexico. In New Mexico, I was asked whether we could teach casino management and land use. Yes, we could, but not if there is federal accountability about algebra and 20 other subjects that make it impossible to fit these subjects in.

SOME SUBJECTS ARE MORE IMPORTANT THAN OTHER SUBJECTS

Yes, we have electives. But they don't matter. Because accountability means making sure that we first teach what does matter. What matters is the stuff that we are holding people accountable for. Since this seems to be math and science these days, for no good reason I can discern, this means that we will get to the stuff that would excite kids and keep them in school, and might teach them some job skills, after we are done with the important stuff. But I am certain that none of the politicians mentioned in the *Times* article knows the quadratic formula or the elements of the periodic table, which is, of course, the stuff of accountability since it is so easy to test. Then how can that be the important stuff?

ALL IMPORTANT SUBJECTS CAN BE EASILY TESTED

Yes, there are right answers in math. But are there right answers in whether we should have invaded Iraq? No? Does that mean we can't teach how governments actually work and how to get reasoned arguments to be heard? Is there a right speech political candidates should make? Does that mean we can't ask students to give speeches because we can't easily assess them? Do we teach only subjects for which there are clear right answers? We do now, which is one reason why school is a deadly experience for one and all and will remain so as long as accountability is the key word in government.

SEEING WHO DID BETTER THAN WHOM IN SCHOOL IS AN INTRINSIC PART OF THE EDUCATIONAL PROCESS

It really is all about competition, isn't it? Bush, both Clintons, and Obama are all the winners of the school competition. They went to Ivy League schools, which seems to be the real issue for most parents. I taught at Ivy League schools and I was profoundly unimpressed with the test-taking, grade-grubbing students I found there. The goal of education is not to say who won, and it is not to tell Harvard whom to admit. The goal is provide real-world skills, some of which may not be so easy to assess until the graduate actually shows up in the real world.

ALL CHILDREN HAVE THE SAME EDUCATIONAL NEEDS

There is more than a 50% dropout rate in many high schools because we have forgotten that not everyone is going to Harvard and that going to Harvard is not the goal of education. Some children simply need to learn about ethics and business and child raising and how the legal system works, how to take care of their health and how to understand when politicians are saying things that make no sense. Why wouldn't those subjects be critical? No politician seems to think any of those are more important than math and science. How about the student who has a passion for the environment, or doing social good, or being a good parent, or running for office? Does every student's school life have to be the same?

STUDENTS LEARN THAT MEMORIZATION IS MORE IMPORTANT THAN THINKING

In an answer-obsessed world, "go figure it out for yourself" or "go try it and see what happens" are replaced by more memorization. Giving kids a chance to fail helps them learn. Actively preventing failure by telling the right answer just helps kids pass tests. In each of the cognitive processes that I presented in Chapter 4, failure is a natural part of the learning process. One's first hypothesis will be wrong. One will plan badly or botch a negotiation. These processes are all about failure, not right answers. Recovering from failure, getting better next time, is what learning is all about. Learning entails failure and cannot happen without it. The kind of failure I have in mind here is expectation failure. This means that we can fail even when we succeed, because we didn't expect things to happen quite like they did. Our predictions are often wrong. We work at getting better at making them and explaining to ourselves why we were wrong. This process of expectation failure followed by explanation is at the heart of learning. That's what learning is all about. Memorization has nothing whatever to do with learning, unless you want to become a singer.

How can we offer new curricula and new ways of learning if no matter what we do children must pass algebra tests? Each administration says over and over again that science is important, but since science in high school is defined for the most part by boring tests of vocabulary terms and definitions, who would be excited to learn science? If a really good scientific reasoning curriculum were created, the schools could not offer it unless it helped kids pass the very same tests that that curriculum was intended to replace.

We must make radical change. The only way to do that is to stop focusing on teaching subjects and stop using the fact-based tests are the natural end result of that focus on subjects.

An education system based on cognitive processes would look very different indeed.

CHAPTER 8

New Curricula for a New Way of Teaching

> A smart man makes a mistake, learns from it, and never makes that mistake again. But a wise man finds a smart man and learns from him how to avoid the mistake altogether.
>
> —Roy H. Williams

How do we put all this into practice? First, let's make sure we avoid creating departments around each of the 12 cognitive processes. The organization around subjects, which is the basis of how our schools are organized, is the source of the problem in both universities and high schools.

Subjects create departments. Departments in universities are a serious problem for students and administrators. They represent silos where decisions are made that will help the department prosper. Departments lobby for their courses to be required so they can hire more faculty. They make sure majors in their departments follow certain rules for graduation that are intended to make students scholars in their field rather than practitioners. Departments are the reason students graduate without job skills. Faculty are almost always against practical training. English departments have to be forced to teach students to write. Computer science departments have to be forced to teach students to program in a way that would make them hirable by industry. Psychology departments avoid teaching clinical psychology, which is really what students what to learn more about.

For about 10 years I have been building new online story-centered curricula. The idea behind a story-centered curriculum (SCC) is that a good curriculum should tell a story. That story should be one in which the student plays one or more roles. Those roles should be those that normally come up in such a story. These curricula are intended to teach students how to actually do something. The roles students play in the story are ones that a graduate of such a program actually might do in real life or actually might need to know about (possibly because he is likely to manage or work with someone who performs that role).

Stories have been at the center of human consciousness for a long time. People tell stories, and the stories they tell shape who they are. People hear stories and remember those that resonate deeply with them. And, people live stories. The stories they live become part of them in a deep way. While we may easily forget everything about a traditional course we took in high school, we can hardly forget the roles we have played in real-life experiences, especially when those roles went on for a long time and had emotional impact on us.

The central argument here is that good education requires good stories—not solely stories that one is told, however. A good education relies on the creation of stories that a student can participate in and feel deeply about. This means that those stories must include others who are playing roles the student will have to deal with on the job, and that the roles the student plays in the stories must relate to the current or future roles that the student intends to play in his or her career.

The SCC is inherently goal-based. The goals must be those that a student has already. For small boys, for example, it can be assumed that the idea of building a truck or designing an airplane is an activity that would grab their interest. For older students, these would be ones like current or future job assignments. In an online world, it is quite possible to create hundreds or thousands of choices and allow students to pick what they want to do—not what they want to study, but activities that genuinely excite them.

The SCC is inherently activity-based. The tasks that constitute the SCC must relate to goals that the student has and the tasks that people actually perform in the roles that the student will play when the training is completed. Thus, an SCC is made up of a set of real-life types of tasks that make up the bulk of the work done by the student, and a set of events that occasionally interrupt or augment those tasks.

Thanks to a grant from the Kauffman Foundation, we built a full-year (all day, every day) high school curriculum in health sciences. This would be, ideally, used in a high school that offered perhaps over 100 full-year curricula. Students would choose four that they liked and after completing them would graduate from high school. All of the curricula would teach what it is like to live in a part of the real world, as well as allowing for practice in the 12 cognitive processes. It takes a while to build these SCCs and they are quite expensive to build, but they cost less than building a new school, so the money could easily be made available.

Let's look at the health sciences curriculum we built.

The year in health sciences comprises nine "rotations," each lasting 3 to 4 full-time weeks on average, in which students experience what it is like to solve the kinds of problems real professionals solve in various specialized fields related to biology and healthcare. These experiences are set in realistic stories in which the students play a leading role. The rotations are conducted consecutively. Students primarily work on assigned projects in teams, although each rotation has independent tasks as well. Each of the rotations was created with the assistance of an expert in each of the respective specialties.

One goal of the curriculum is for students to discover that practicing science is fun and relevant to real-world problems. They also should develop a sense of what it would be like to work as a practitioner in the various health sciences fields, so they can decide whether they might someday like a career in healthcare or biology. Of course, the real goal is to enable practice in the 12 cognitive processes. Let's see how that happens.

The rotations in the year in health sciences are:

1. *Internal Medicine*—Students diagnose and develop a treatment plan for a fictional patient who has a major illness and ultimately requires an organ transplant as a part of his treatment. Students also make judgments about ethical issues related to transplants, following a principled approach to ethical reasoning.

2. *Nutrition Advisor*—Students coach fictional nutritional advisors on their management of teenage clients' nutritional concerns and issues. During the process they also develop nutritional plans for themselves and for a peer.

3. *Super Worm*—Students work for a fictional philanthropic billionaire who asks them to invent ways of modifying the common earthworm so it can more efficiently improve soil to better supply the world with food.

4. *Sports Medic*—Students diagnose and develop treatment plans for patients who have sports-related injuries. In the process students produce in-depth reports on additional issues related to sports medicine.

5. *Designer Genes*—Students consider ethical and political issues related to genetic engineering, for example, cloning, gene therapies, and the manufacturing of drugs. In the process they learn about DNA and the basics of genetic engineering.

6. *Plant Plague*—Students working for a fictional county farming agency are faced with an anomalous powdery mildew that has infected wheat in their local area. They investigate how the new strain of mildew arose and how it spread to this area and crop in particular. They work to develop a treatment for the current crop; then they develop a way to alter the wheat or the way in which it is grown to prevent future fungal outbreaks.

7. *Medical Detective*—Students work with the fictional county medical examiner to conduct medical investigations. They are asked to determine the time and cause of death for various mysterious cases.

8. *Cutting Costs Without Cutting Care*—In this rotation, students consider business aspects related to healthcare. Students play the role of a hospital consultant whose job it is to discern why the hospital is losing money and make recommendations for correcting the situation. In the process they confront ethical issues related to cutting costs in the area of healthcare.

9. *Outbreak*—In this rotation, students work in the areas of infectious disease, epidemiology, and public health administration. They begin by diagnosing the cause of a fictional patient's infection that stems from bacteria in a food item. They then learn that many people across the country have been found with similar illnesses. Students have to develop a plan to manage the outbreak due to the availability of the food item to a wide population. Later they are fictionally hired to develop a readiness plan for a possible worldwide pandemic.

Students spend weeks in each rotation. What do they learn?

Remember, the answer cannot be that they learn about health sciences. Why not?

Because that is really not the issue. No high school student learning a subject really learns that subject. Students forget what they have learned in a day or in a week or a year. Professors always assume that entering high school students need to be retaught the basics. They may pick up the general idea but in reality the content of the subject area is, at best, vaguely understood. What they can learn is that they like a subject or have an interest in learning more.

The only other thing they can learn involves the 12 cognitive processes. So let's look at how the health sciences curriculum covers these processes.

By explicit design, all of the health science rotations emphasize all four of the "social processes." The students work in teams (*teamwork*), sometimes even in collaboration with other teams. The students and teams necessarily try to *influence* one another, *negotiate* with one another, and constantly have to *describe* their points of view and their results. The step-by-step instructions that are part of every rotation explicitly discuss how best to handle this. Now let's look at four of the rotations in detail.

INTERNAL MEDICINE

The essence of this rotation is learning about how to do diagnosis, in this case, of liver disease. Students watch a detailed interview with the patient, select (after some orientation) specific tests to administer, receive the results, and report suggested diagnoses. They must communicate what they have discovered. So they describe the patient's symptoms and must analyze and discuss the causation of the patient's symptoms. Then they begin to plan a course of action. Planning what to do is a major component of this rotation. To do this they must make a judgment as a crucial part of the diagnostic work. They must do this again as well in the ethics unit that occurs later in this rotation. In that unit they undertake a detailed study of both medical and ethical issues in liver transplantation—which is where evaluation comes into play. Here the students become consciously aware of their values as they decide how to influence medical and ethical choices.

SUPER WORM

The students plan carefully for this unit (a hypothetical redesign of the earthworm to make it even more helpful in agriculture). Hypothetical experimentation is performed repeatedly as the students predict the effects of various modifications of the worm's anatomy. Describing their conclusions is important—the project's goals; the worm's anatomy, physiology, and behavior; and the interaction of anatomy and function.

SPORTS MEDIC

The core of this rotation is four athletic injuries. In each case the students examine the patients, describe their observations in detail, and perform a formal differential diagnosis. The students must use judgment and modeling to predict the effect of providing a competitive athlete with an artificial bone implant.

DESIGNER GENES

This rotation has three primary activities. In all three, evaluation plays a role as they discuss genetically modified animals, crops, and muscles. Describing, planning, and influence all are involved as the students prepare a congressman for hearings. All four of the social processes come into play in formal debates.

What should be clear here is that what the health sciences curriculum seems to be about and what it is actually about are very different things. It seems to be about teaching health sciences content, when what it is really about is having students practice various cognitive processes that occur again and again throughout life. This was the goal of the design, pure and simple: to help students practice thinking. It really doesn't matter what arena they are thinking in. We get them interested in thinking by having them think about something that interests them and is connected to a world they may wish to explore later on in life. They may indeed learn something about that world as well, but the point is the cognitive process-based education, not the subject-based education.

I thought of the idea of building SCCs instead of using the normal set of courses that constitute most students' school year when I took a job with Carnegie Mellon University (CMU) as the Chief Education Officer of its new West Coast campus, located in Silicon Valley. There were no faculty located at this campus, since Carnegie Mellon is in Pittsburgh. I took this as an opportunity, not as a problem, since faculty want to teach the way they always have taught. Lecturing is easy and faculty like to do it. Students have learned to cope with lecturing and later cramming for tests, so no one complains much. No one learns much from this, but no one seems to be too concerned about it.

I was asked to design master's degree programs in computer science. It seemed to me that students entered a master's degree program because they wanted to get a good job after graduation, so I asked what jobs they were preparing for as I looked at each Pittsburgh campus program. Even though the faculty in Pittsburgh had been teaching these master's degree programs for years, faculty members were surprisingly unconcerned with what students did after graduation. They just taught their courses, their specialties actually, and assumed the students would find value in them. This seemed an odd state of affairs to anyone who looked at it from the outside, but as professor I know that faculty are rarely concerned with master's degree students at all and naturally wouldn't have given these programs that much thought.

There was a great deal of hostility to the SCCs that were built by my team and me. They were seen as threatening the existing structure of courses and lectures. Nevertheless, the students liked them a great deal and the people who mentored in them, after some initial resistance, began to like them and promote them. This happened in the areas of software engineering and software development.

The faculty in e-business liked what we had built so much that they got rid of the existing course-based, e-business master's degree they had offered in Pittsburgh and now offer only the SCC version on the main CMU campus.

SCCs work and work well. Students learn actual skills and teachers feel like they are helping students do something real. But faculty, who are used to the old classroom-style method, often resist doing the hard work now required of them. This is true for students as well. One mentor in the West Coast e-business program who himself had graduated from the Pittsburgh classroom-based program said that he felt sorry for the kids on the West Coast campus because they had to work so hard. He noted that they were learning a lot more than he did but that he had liked sitting in the back of the classroom and ignoring the teacher. It was much easier and he had done well at that.

A story-centered curriculum is intended to teach cognitive processes, not subjects. Subjects are, of course, covered, but they are not really the point. Certain things need to be done again and again in life, but those things can be learned only in context, not as an abstraction. Different contexts must be provided in order to motivate students and to provide real-world skills that will be remembered, not because they were studied and tested, but because they were practiced again and again.

What is life like in a story-centered curriculum? The first ones we built were built as master's degree programs at Carnegie Mellon's new West Coast campus. Here is Max Soderby, a mentor in the first one of those master's programs, talking about his experience:

> I am almost jealous in a way because I see that they are gaining skills more rapidly than I gained them when I was a student in Pittsburgh at CMU's campus. They get exposure to things that we just talked about in a lecture hall, whereas they are actually doing it: implementing actual software and putting designs into practice. We mostly did homework and talked about it in a lecture hall. So I am jealous in that respect. It is also a lot more work, but that work pays off for the students.

Subject-based education is not really supposed to be training for work. I once proposed to the president of Yale (Bart Giamatti) that we build a master's degree program in an area of computer science that would help get people jobs after graduation. He said that that was training and that Yale does not do training. The academic subjects taught at Yale are meant to produce scholars. But, in a way, he was very wrong. Yale does do training. Yale and almost all other colleges are divided into departments, and a major in a department's subject typically is seen by the faculty as preparation for an academic career in that subject.

The students may well have a different point of view, however. Unfortunately, they come away disappointed. An English major could be hoping to become a journalist, but the education that he will receive is more likely to be appropriate for creating an English professor. A math major may well want to be an actuary, but will not learn actuarial science at Yale. He will learn to be a potential mathematics professor. And, worst of all, in my own field of computer science, the very idea that a Yale degree would make you capable of getting a good job as a programmer is frowned upon by the faculty. They are training computer science professors. This is the logical end result of subject-based training.

Now, what Giamatti had in mind as the end goal of college, training for the mind, is a noble enough ideal, and a natural outcome of cognitive process-based education. The classic liberal arts view of education, one that a reader might think I am not in favor of, is actually a better model than the model that has evolved in the nation's top universities. The idea that you should try thinking in a variety of fields is a better plan, and one more in line with what I am proposing here, than the model that exists on most universities' campuses. The latter model, the one that makes students major in a subject and thus supposedly become prepared to work in that field, is really just a big lie.

There is nothing unusual here. Here again, is a statement from the Ivy League professor whom I quoted earlier:

> There is an unspoken rule at places like my university that if you are really good, you do exactly what your teacher does.

So what are these schools training students for? It could be only one thing—to become professors. There is no attempt to teach practical real-world applications of the ideas taught in classes, in part because the faculty themselves don't know those applications. Here is the Big Ten computer science professor again:

> There are roughly 60 faculty members in computer science. They cover all the traditional areas of computer science. Ironically, software engineering, which is what 90% of the undergraduates do when they graduate, is not covered. It is not considered an intellectual or academic discipline. It is considered too practical. There is only one software engineering course and it is taught by an adjunct because no one really cares about it.

This is a real problem because (the Big Ten professor again). . .

> There are hundreds of computer science majors here. The faculty doesn't feel it needs to change because there are students

clamoring for what is now offered. Ninety-eight percent of them want to be programmers. Almost none of them want Ph.D.s.

I cannot go to a faculty meeting any more. I get into a fight at every faculty meeting. I argue about teaching and education and they think they know because they are professors. I cannot subject myself anymore to their abuse.

These problems exist precisely because of the subject-based education system. That system is about factual knowledge, and it is this emphasis on factual knowledge that has given rise to the testing mania that has swept the country. These problems exist because the real mission of the university is very different than the general public imagines.

Here is a quote and a story that I rather like:

A university is what a college becomes when the faculty loses interest in students.—John Ciardi

Benjamin Franklin told the story of some Massachusetts commissioners who invited the Indians to send a dozen of their youth to study free at Harvard. The Indians replied that they had sent some of their young braves to study there years earlier, but on their return "they were absolutely good for nothing, being neither acquainted with the true methods for killing deer, catching beaver, or surprising an enemy." They offered instead to educate a dozen or so white children in the ways of the Indians "and make men of them."(From *Benjamin Franklin, An American Life*, by Walter Isaacson)

What has changed? Key life skills no longer include catching beaver. Otherwise, things are pretty much the same. Change "catching beaver" to any modern daily skill, and Franklin's story is just as valid today.

What do students really learn at a great university? Parents never really ask this question. They just know that their kid got into a good college and that their child is lucky to go there.

Should you avoid sending your child to top schools because they don't teach so well there and really don't plan to improve the situation any time soon?

No. Of course not. If your child gets into Yale, send her there. It is a great place. But you should know what Yale actually has to offer and what it doesn't.

If your child wants to be a professor, Yale is the place.
If your child wants to be an intellectual, Yale is the place.
If your child wants to go to law school, Yale is the place.
If your child wants to hobnob with the best and brightest, Yale is the place.
If your child wants to have a fun time for 4 years, Yale is the place.

Then what is wrong?

There is a problem only if you think that there is a different reason to go to college than the reasons I have listed above.

Oh. There is this other problem. Many of the other 3,000 colleges are trying very hard to imitate Yale. They attempt to provide similar experiences and they can't pull it off. Yale is a unique place. The nation can afford only so many unique places, however. We cannot afford having the main university of a state thinking it is Yale, as my state university friend suggests. If every university has as its main focus research and not education, then the best and brightest of each state will be trained, not necessarily willingly, to be academics rather than practitioners. There will be a great many students who came to school for an education that will help them in their future lives who will be disappointed to find out that that is not the type of education being offered.

Professors at Yale are playing the prestige game. Unfortunately, they are hardly alone in this.

My state university professor again:

We definitely want to be part of the superstar system but we have no superstars. If we had them, we would probably lose them to Harvard and Yale anyway. Nevertheless, we are obsessed with the National Rankings put out by places like *U.S. News and World Report*. Faculty and deans say they are not obsessed with them, but rankings are an important part of the evaluation process and shape a department's growth. We want to be in the top 4 or 5 universities. We are not but that's what we want to be.

U.S. News and World Report's annual rankings weigh heavily on the minds of the faculty and administration of universities who are in the prestige game. These rankings are based on numbers: average SAT scores of admitted students, average rank in class of admitted students, faculty publications, and many other numbers that come out in favor of research universities with world-class faculty. But world-class faculty means faculty who care about research and not about teaching. While there certainly is no harm in going to Harvard or Yale, the success of their students hardly depends on what they learned in those places and depends a great deal more on the fact that the best and the brightest are the ones who go there in the first place.

These places get away with teaching courses in obscure issues in literature and history, or in economic theory or in complex mathematics, by pretending that they are really teaching students to think. But does knowing obscure information necessarily imply that one is a good thinker?

A good thinker, I claim, would be good at each of the 12 cognitive processes.

What does it mean to be good at prediction, for example? Is a 2-year-old good at prediction? Is a dog good at prediction? Is a professional gambler good at prediction? Is a stock trader good at prediction? Is a mother of a toddler good at prediction? Is a politician good at prediction? Is a scientist good at prediction?

We actually are quite good at assessing the ability of others at prediction precisely because we have data to support our conclusions. We know how good gamblers or stock traders are at predicting. If they are very successful, we can say they are brilliant at what they do, or we can say they are lucky. Those are our choices.

The same is true of scientists. Most scientists make predictions, and those that are proven right are seen as brilliant. Luck enters into science as well and quite often scientists say that a given Nobel Prize winner was lucky and isn't really all that bright.

Dogs are seen as being smart (for a dog) when they can correctly predict the arrival of their master or bad weather or threats, and are seen as stupid when they bark at thunder. Their behavior is seen as stupid precisely because of the erroneous prediction that barking will scare the thunder away. A dog's inability to predict is exactly why we think dogs are dumb animals, and when they surprise us with an accurate prediction, they are seen as smart. Of course, we don't expect dogs to predict who will win the big game. We know their limitations.

But it is not only the accuracy of predictions that factors into our sense of a person's or an animal's ability to think. We say that a person is intelligent even when he predicts badly, if he gives good explanations for his predictions even though they don't pan out.

So when a sportscaster gives his prediction about the outcome of an upcoming game, we think he is intelligent if he has thought it out carefully, and if his explanation is coherent, and if his reasoning is sound, and we give extra credit if some of his ideas are surprising in some way. So, even if he subsequently turns out to be wrong, we still think he is good at thinking.

But prediction is actually quite complicated to judge. We respect great predictors. We think people who can predict well, especially those who can explain their predictions well, are very intelligent. But, often, we see intelligence when it may not be there. The reason is scripts. And we may fail to see it when it is there. The reason for that is explanations.

Scripts and explanations are at the beginning and at the end of intelligent behavior. What do I mean by that?

When a child is learning about the world, she is learning the scripts that commonly are followed in the world that she inhabits. I have explained this at length in two different books,[1] so I will just summarize here.

Scripts tell us what will happen next in the aspects of the world that repeat frequently. Anyone who goes to a restaurant knows that when you order food, someone will bring it to you and later you will be expected to pay for it. There are lots of variations on this standard restaurant script, however. It doesn't work quite like that at Burger King. The script is different but there is a script there too and we learn it if we frequent Burger King. The restaurant script has many variations and we are initially confused when we encounter a new one, but we learn through repeated practice. And, we generalize so that we can understand that the McDonald's script is pretty much the same as the one at Burger King.

We can predict what will happen next in the world based on experiences we have repeated. Following scripts is so normal that it is not seen as a sign of intelligence to be able to do it. We don't exclaim: Wow, he predicted that the waitress would bring what we ordered and she did. Amazing!

But the opposite is certainly seen as a sign of stupidity. Once one has experienced something many times, one should know what will happen next in that arena. Dogs usually know the scripts that pertain to them, as well. They know which merchant will have the dog biscuit for them, for example.

People seem astonishingly dumb when they can't predict what is obvious to everyone else. Not knowing what will happen next in a script you don't know, because you don't have the relevant experience, means nothing at all, of course. The question is: If you have experienced something repeatedly, why haven't you figured out that what you have seen before will happen again?

Script following is, therefore, a sign of intelligence but a very limited one. We can blindly follow a script, and this can make us seem dumb indeed. Since scripts vary one from the other in many ways, the ability to see the nuances makes all the difference. Expecting that a fast-food restaurant will be the same as a three-star Michelin restaurant because it is a restaurant after all is what makes people seem stupid. Failing to make the right generalizations indicates a lack of thought.

The real question is this: What do you do when your script fails? This is important because scripts fail all the time. You expect something to happen and it doesn't. You love the cheesecake at Lindy's and suddenly it doesn't serve cheesecake. Or you find that Lindy's is now out of business. What do you do? People recover from script failure on a daily basis. How they do this tells us a lot about how the mind works.

When people refuse to abandon the generalizations they have made, they immediately are perceived as being stupid. When a medical assistant asked me the other day about the upcoming Thanksgiving holiday, I responded that I would be eating duck instead of turkey. She said that sounded awful and that duck was greasy and gamey and it sounded like a terrible idea. I asked her if she had ever eaten duck and she said no because it was game and she hated game. I told her it wasn't gamey. She refused to believe me. I was about to recommend trying magret de canard but thought better of it and asked if she had ever eaten in a French restaurant in her life. She said that she hadn't.

People who have scripts often generalize them so that in their own minds they are experts on things that they have never experienced. This is what stupid looks like.

On the other hand, we might wonder what smart looks like. Let's imagine the same woman with the same beliefs hearing me say that duck was not gamey or greasy. Intelligent people respond, when they are confused, or when a long-held belief is challenged, with a request for evidence. She might have asked where she might try duck or what duck tasted like since she had not understood it correctly. She might have allowed for the possibility that she was wrong and asked to know more. But she didn't. People who aren't intellectually curious rarely do.

This kind of dull thinking is not so much a matter of genetics as it is a matter of not having been educated properly. And, that is, of course, the real issue here. If a child grows up in a world where questions are expected and where long-held beliefs can be abandoned because of new evidence, he will seek such interactions. But a child who grows up in a world where adults set themselves up as knowing everything and no one's beliefs are ever questioned, you will get mindless behavior like this.

Of course, it doesn't matter if this woman doesn't try duck. It is likely, however, that this behavior pattern—learn rules and never question them—pervades her life. This leads me to my main point.

Scripts are great things to have. They get you through the airport. They get you through Burger King. They get you through most of the mundane aspects of life. But scripts need to be modified. They fail all the time. The airport starts a new check-in procedure. The restaurant you always go to deletes your favorite item from the menu. The store you always shop in is getting very crowded. At some point we encounter script failure and we deal with it. The question is how.

We deal with script failure using two key procedures. It is our facility with these procedures that differentiates intelligence from stupidity. Thinking depends on them, and everyone must do them when trying to think. But not everyone does them well.

The procedures are:

Generalization
Explanation

These are not new ideas in the context of this book. Explanation is one kind of describing. Generalization is the method by which we do prediction, make judgments, do diagnosis, and determine causation. We generalize whenever we try to think.

This entire book is a generalization. It is an attempt to make sense of a vast array of information. That is what generalization is all about. The book is also an explanation of the generalizations I have found to be true. At the core of thinking, you find generalization and explanation. But it is important to remember that what starts the process of generalization and explanation is failure. Without failure we don't try to generalize and explain because we have nothing to generalize and explain. Thinking, therefore, looks like this:

> Make a prediction
> Prediction fails
> Make a generalization
> Explain your generalization
> Make a new prediction

Let me explain how this works and why one cannot think well if one cannot do this. To explain, I will tell a personal story relating to my own thinking and learning with respect to two of the twelve cognitive processes. I will explain afterwards why I have chosen to tell stories and why I have used personal ones.

DESCRIBING

Let's start with describing. There is, of course, an art to describing. Anyone who writes and anyone who speaks publicly is learning all the time about describing. Since I was a professor for 30 odd years, and since I have written hundreds of papers and about 25 books, and since I have given numerous keynote speeches around the world, I have been thinking a great deal about describing for many years. I learn something whenever I speak publicly because I can easily tell whether I am being heard or not. Are the listeners on the edge of their seats or are they half asleep (or literally asleep)? I learn when I write because I read the reviews, and colleagues are always happy to tell me what was wrong with what I wrote.

Once, I was given a lesson in public speaking by someone older and wiser than me that I never forgot. I recently had been hired at Stanford as a professor. I was pretty young (22) and full of myself. In those days, the Computer Science Department ran a course for new graduate students that served as an introduction to all the special research possibilities in artificial intelligence for those who wanted to enter that field. There were many faculty in AI at Stanford and each got a week to talk about what his work was about. The goal was to try to convince students to sign up for a special research seminar with that faculty member the following quarter.

My champion at Stanford was a psychiatrist named Kenneth Colby. He invited me to share his week and thus we would be a team for which students could sign up the following quarter. I listened to his talks to the students. He was very funny but rather light on content, in my opinion. I wasn't impressed. But, after I spoke, he said something to me I never forgot. He said: If you try to say everything that you know in an hour, either of two things is true. Either you can do it and therefore you must not know very much, or else you can't do it and you will talk way too fast trying to fit it all in and you will be generally incomprehensible.

I listened to what he had to say, but I wasn't sure he was right. At the first meeting of our jointly run seminar, we discovered that we had won the student jackpot. While other faculty had gotten four or five sign-ups, we had gotten 25. I was very proud of myself until the students went around the table to say who they were and why they had signed up. Not a single one of them had signed up because of anything I had said. They had been mesmerized by Colby.

Then I reheard in my head what Colby had told me the previous quarter. He had entertained them—not overwhelmed them. They thought he would be interesting and fun and they wanted to work with him. While I had looked down on his lighthearted presentation style, it turned out he knew what he was doing.

So, what did I learn and how did my thinking change? Thinking, as I said earlier, looks like this:

Make a prediction
Prediction fails
Make a generalization
Explain your generalization
Make a new prediction

What was my prediction? I had predicted that speaking quickly with a great deal of brilliant content would woo the incoming students. This was simply wrong. I needed to make a new generalization. Fortunately, I did not have to do the work myself. Colby had helped me by supplying a generalization that he believed to be true. (Good teachers do exactly this: They supply generalizations when a student needs one and cannot come up with one by himself after a prediction that he made has failed.)

The generalization that Colby supplied was, more or less: Be entertaining if you want to attract followers and be listened to.

Was he right? Is this a good generalization?

The next step in thinking is: Explain your generalization. What this means here is that I needed to understand why this might be true. If possible, one wants to test out the new hypothesis. Fortunately for me, I had many opportunities to speak in public over the next 40 years. I tried many different methods of teaching and lecturing. Entertaining always works. Colby was right.

But I said that one needs to explain why it works. This is my explanation: People have trouble paying attention to someone who talks for an hour. Human beings are not built for this. Our ancestors certainly didn't listen to lectures. People communicate best by asking questions and interrupting. Since this isn't possible in a lecture, any questions they might ask, they ask themselves and try to answer. While they are thinking about what a speaker says, the speaker keeps on talking. No one can really hear a lecture, in my opinion. So, a good speaker, recognizing this, does not try to make the audience do that. He makes them laugh, he paints interesting pictures for them to ponder, he amazes them perhaps, but he does not try to get them to, nor does he expect them to, remember all that he has said. The less content, the more likely they will remember. Colby knew all this. I learned it over time. He jump-started my thinking.

By now, this new generalization of mine, together with my explanation, is part of my core beliefs. But any belief can be challenged by reality. And, any new belief generates new predictions. So I predicted that if I was funnier when I spoke, people would appreciate what I said more. I also predicted that if I didn't speak much in a graduate seminar and let students argue with one another, they would get more out of it. After 40 years I still believe these things. But, and this is the important part, there are nuances upon nuances about all these issues in my memory. I need to explain it simply when I write or speak about it, but when I think about it, I recall all kinds of exceptions and caveats. I know, or at least I think I know, a great deal about speaking and have lots of memories about specific successes and failures. Thinking and learning require one to recall one's experiences, analyze those experiences, come up with new hypotheses about failures, make new predictions, and be prepared for these predictions to fail. This is what thinking looks like no matter which cognitive process is being thought about and practiced.

DIAGNOSIS

Now let's talk about diagnosis. Again I will start with a story. This is one I have been telling for a long time because it informs us about how the mind works.

I was discussing with my colleague (Bob Abelson) how it could be that my wife could not seem to make steak rare (as I like it—she is no longer my wife, but not because of this). Bob responded that he couldn't get his hair cut as short as he wanted in England 20 years earlier.

This seems on the surface to be a rather odd response, but when we look deeper we can see that I was saying something like, She could do this right if she wanted to, and he was thinking, Maybe she thinks the request is too extreme, as happened to me with a barber in England many years ago.

Matching odd situations to other odd situations and seeing the similarity is what creative thinking is all about. Bob was trying to diagnose a problem that had been on his mind for a long time, and my new story provided him with new evidence to think again about what the proper diagnosis might be. This is what thinking looks like. It is also what reminding looks like. People get reminded precisely because they are trying to match a new situation to one they already know about and thereby determine what to do next. To put this another way, diagnosis depends on prior diagnosis. We constantly are trying to improve our diagnostic capability because we always strive to make better decisions no matter what arena these decisions are in. The fact that the improvement of diagnostic capability is not explicitly part of each and every curriculum in school is scandalous.

When we design new curricula, we need to ground them in some realistic framework that will enable students to practice things that they might end up doing in the real world. But that does not mean that the real issue in designing these curricula is anything other than teaching thinking, that is, enabling practice in the 12 cognitive processes. However, teaching thinking in the absence of a context that truly interests students is absurd.

CHAPTER 9

How to Teach the Twelve Cognitive Processes That Underlie Learning

The art of teaching is the art of assisting discovery.
—Mark Van Doren

We need to completely redefine what we mean by school and what we do in school. We need to think about education in a new way. Rather than wanting people to be educated, which usually means being able to quote Shakespeare or nod sagely when Freud's name is mentioned, we need to expect people to be able to think well. Education would be better defined by defining an educated person as one who can make well-reasoned arguments for what they are about to do.

We must focus on teaching cognitive processes and abandoning the subject-based (and test-based) education system we have now that is clearly failing. The reason we have all those tests is simply because we have no idea how to make people learn all the stuff that is part of that subject-based system without threatening them. No one really wants to learn the Pythagorean theorem or information about the Taft Hartley Act. Let scholars know about these things; the average person just doesn't need to know this stuff.

But people do know how to find and use the mathematics they need when they have continually practiced it, and they know how to find prior relevant experiences when they have to come up with a new plan they want to propose. That simply does not mean we have to tell it all to them years before they might ever make use of it.

In the age of the Internet, just-in-time learning is a serious reality. We can change things now in part because we have information readily available online. But the Internet has been designed by committee. It has much in it that is nonsense, and finding what you need just in time can be quite difficult. Still, it would not be that complicated to design a different kind of Internet, the moral equivalent of *Encyclopedia*

Britannica, if you will. It would be filled with knowledge from experts that had been vetted by other experts and delivered seamlessly without your having to search for it. You don't need to be a scholar in order to make reasoned decisions. You just need to know how to find information to help you think things out well. This means that learning to think clearly and knowing how to assess the value of new evidence that one has found, must be the main goal of any school system.

When does school start to falter? One way to think about school is to ask about the significance and age-related properties of each of the cognitive processes. Let's see if we can rank the processes in terms of age. Which of these processes would we expect a child who was entering school to already be able to do? To put this another way, a normal 5-year-old:

1. can make some accurate predictions about very simple things, like where his mother might be and what she might be doing and what will be on television
2. would have trouble modeling any process
3. has a limited sense of evaluation but knows what he likes
4. would be able to experiment with simple things like food and toys
5. might be able to do limited diagnosis of what might have gone wrong in a process, but it typically would be limited to explanations that he had heard from someone else
6. might be able to do limited planning based on plans that had been used before
7. might know something about causation because he would have been told about it and remembered what he had been told
8. can make some judgments based on his own tastes and what he has been taught about what is good and what is bad
9. can do some describing, but typically is not at all good at it
10. should be able to influence some people, especially his grandparents
11. should be able to work in a simple team together with kids his own age toward a goal
12. should be able to do some simple negotiation, especially with his parents, siblings, and some friends

So, upon reaching school age, a child can do some of the cognitive processes. Now the question is, How to we teach him to get better at them?

First let's see what the cognitive processes fundamentally have in common. This will give us a way of thinking about how to teach them.

The first and most important thing they have in common is that they all rely on a case base. We have all engaged in each of these processes many times, and we have a range of experiences we can call upon to guide us the next time we find ourselves doing them. Each process relies on a story base as well. We can tell stories about interesting experiences we have had in doing each one of them. Stories usually revolve around failures, or at least unexpected results, since without these there are no good stories to tell. Engaging in any cognitive process includes the possibility of making a mistake during the process. We expect to get smarter each time as a result of any mistakes we make. This is what cognitive processes are like. We learn cognitive processes through experience, and we index the failures we have so that we can find them again and perhaps avoid making the same mistake. When we avoid an error that we know we have made previously, we say that we have learned.

It follows, therefore, that acquiring a case base, learning the stories of others and learning to tell our own stories, and learning classic mistakes and being able to analyze behavior to find a mistake are all aspects of learning the cognitive processes.

Acquiring the case base and consciously analyzing the cases in that case base, then, is the fundamental issue in teaching the cognitive processes.

HOW TO TEACH PREDICTION

We live in a physical world but we also live in a social world. Children need to understand that if they drop something heavy on their foot, it will hurt; they also need to know that if they do something mean to someone, the person may dislike them for it and may seek revenge. We use predictions to figure out what will happen as a result of our actions and then we use that knowledge to guide us in our future actions. What kinds of predictions do children regularly make, then? And, what can we teach and how can they learn?

1. Children predict the actions of the people that they interact with, but they do not necessarily realize that they do this.
2. Children predict the reactions of objects and actions in the physical world, but they do not necessarily realize that they do this either.
3. Children predict their own feelings and mental states. They do things that they think will make them happy, but they don't necessarily realize that they do this either.

These three worlds, the social, the physical, and the mental, are at the center of what adults make predictions about. We predict the speed of an oncoming car and decide whether we can cross the street safely. Children may not do this so well. We predict what will happen when we scream and yell at someone, but children may not predict this too well either. We predict events that will make us happy or sad, such as taking a nice vacation, or playing a game, or a good meal, or establishing a relationship with another person. Children do not consciously think about such things.

But adults do think about these things, so where do children learn about them? At the present time, the answer is that they learn about them as events happen randomly in their lives. If they are lucky enough to have someone helpful to talk with about their experiences, they may, in fact, become good at analyzing how the world works and making their predictions conscious. Getting better at prediction is the cornerstone of living one's life in a satisfying way. One can, of course, get better at prediction by simply thinking about it—this is how most people do that today, of course. But not everyone is capable of doing that and, clearly, most adults are not all that good at making important predictions in their own lives. (This is one reason that there are bad marriages, financial counselors, clinical psychologists, and prisons.)

What helps teach one to predict is to hear about the experience of others and to be able to reflect on one's own experience. This means that having experiences to reflect upon, and people who are knowledgeable to discuss those experiences with, is at the cornerstone of learning to predict effectively.

This should start as early as 1st grade (or age 5—I don't really believe in grades).

How do we do it? We design experiences for children that are age appropriate and talk about what will happen in those experiences before they do them and how they can learn from and improve upon those experiences after they happen. Then they undergo a slightly more complex experience that builds on what they learned. The process is simple enough. The question is what experiences to design, how to design them.[2]

I should note that prediction is used as a teaching methodology in schools today, especially in reading. I suggested this in a book I wrote about teaching reading in 1978, and since that time (not necessarily because of that book) it has become more common to use prediction to teach reading. Also, high school kids are asked to make predictions in courses that cover current events. Kids predict sporting events or the sex of their in utero sibling.

The idea that kids can make predictions is not a really radical point. My point is that prediction has to be the curriculum, not be ancillary to the curriculum. If we want children to predict well, we need to help them do that. As it stands now, they are on their own. As adults who have not been taught to predict well, they will make poor life decisions, predicting wrongly about how people in their lives (bosses, spouses, children, co-workers, etc.) will behave toward them after they take certain actions, for example. Yes, understanding is improved if one predicts the future actions of characters in a book one is reading—it helps a lot. And, reading is a skill that is very important. But it also helps to understand how to predict daily actions better and how to find out whether you were right and how to explain why you were wrong. Doing this consistently makes you better at predicting something more important than what an author has a character do in a story.

How do we get good at making predictions about the outcome of actions? What outcomes do we need to predict?

Every action we take involves a prediction. When we put one foot in front of the other in an effort to move our bodies forward, we are predicting that this will work, that we won't fall down, and that it won't hurt to do this. Sometimes we do fall or it does hurt. We learn this and compensate next time. This is learning in its most basic form. And obviously, we have been learning about walking since we were very small. We keep learning about walking throughout our lives because things change.

Babies predict what will happen when they cry. They don't start out making such predictions. They learn to expect results that they have already experienced. These are scripts, and I have discussed them at length elsewhere.[3] Scripts are acquired naturally as a result of repeated sequences of events. We predict what will happen next because we know the script. Scripts are not normally taught because they are readily acquired from living. But what if you want to teach them? You might want to teach them in a situation where someone's new job is a script and rather than learn that job from repeated experience, there is a desire to jump-start the process by simply teaching the script. How can we do this?

There is also prediction that is not script-based. In other words, there could well be a script but the predictor doesn't know it. How can one learn to predict well if one does not have a script?

And lastly, there is often the need to predict when there couldn't possibly be a script because what needs to be predicted is novel, at least to the predictor. How can the prediction be made? More important, how can someone be taught to predict in that kind of situation?

These, then, are the three aspects of prediction: learning a script; functioning without a script because it isn't known; and predicting when there is no script.

How do we teach these things? Scripts are learned through repetition. No one seeks to explain to a child that since she will be doing something again and again, she will now memorize the steps before she tries it out for the first time. Instead, we take the child through the steps until she has learned them. There is no need to try to teach a child scripts (such as how restaurants function or airplane rides go or school procedure works). We can say some words about these things, of course, but the learning comes from repeated practice no matter what we do.

Teachers (and course designers) often fail to understand about teaching scripts. Talking about what a student will have to do later will not help that student do what he is being asked to do. We don't learn scripts consciously and thus aren't likely to remember what we are consciously told about what to do. We are conscious when we execute a script—we are thinking about what will happen next—but not so much in words as in expectations of next events. We don't talk about one foot going in front of the other foot or think about it very much. So if a teacher tries to teach us about it, it is doubtful that the words will help us much. Scripts are practiced. We can prepare for them if that makes people happy. We can tell a child what will happen when he rides in an airplane for the first time, but it isn't so that he can do what he is supposed to do so much as to make him more comfortable and less surprised by noises or procedures that might be upsetting. The only way to really learn a script is to do it again and again.

So what does this tell us about teaching scripts? What if we don't have the time to allow a student to practice? This is, of course, what happens in job-training situations. We tell someone what to do and hope they very quickly will learn how to do it. We can't afford weeks of practice. So how do we teach scripts in that case?

The answer to this depends on the number of mistakes that it is possible to make while executing a script. The real issue in script execution is, after all, not knowing the next steps, but knowing what to do (or what not to do) when the script begins to falter in some way. This means that a teacher (or a course designer) must have one question in mind when thinking about teaching a script: What are the most common (and most important) mistakes that are made by novices when they execute this script?

To teach people to avoid mistakes in a script, or to teach them to get out of difficult situations properly, one must practice those situations. This means that script teaching must focus around errors and that it is the job of a teacher to systematically make sure that everything that could go wrong, does go wrong in any practice situation. Teaching scripts means helping the student form a case base of errors and a case base of how to handle them. Here again, this cannot be taught consciously. Script failures must be taught through practice. The students must build up their own case bases by experiencing the problem and then either think their way out of it, or learn standard solutions as a way out of it by practicing them. So, we can speed up the script-learning process by creating a simulation that has every important mistake built into it, waiting for the student to trip up and make that mistake.

When a script isn't known and predictions need to be made, the usual human procedure is to adapt on old script to serve as a temporary new one. Never been on a plane but have been on a train? Never been in a fancy restaurant but have been to a fast-food restaurant?

Never been to college but have been to high school? These are situations that happen to people. They usually assume that one is like the other. While this assumption may not work out all that well, it is the best a scriptless person can do in the situation.

A teacher, therefore, can take advantage of this human desire to see unknown A as being like known B. People do this all the time. They assume the girl they just met will behave like the last one they went out with. They assume that their teacher will behave the way their last teacher did. They assume that their new car works the way the last one did. They do this with situations as well. What it means is that people predict on the basis of experience, and it is the job of the teacher to help students understand which of their prior experiences is most relevant when they are confused. Doing this is not so easy. But it is possible and it is a proper area for a teacher or a course to focus on.

Here is the process. Students need to be asked what to do in a situation that is new to them. Their natural response would be to rely on prior experience. The teacher's job is to make that reliance explicit. To ask students to say which experience they will rely on for help in the new situation and ask why they think that that particular choice will be helpful. To ask them to analyze the differences between the current issue and the prior script and to predict where the prior script might not work. To ask them to think of alternative scripts that might help.

What I have described here is the basic process of indexing cases and matching cases, which is critical to thinking—especially original thinking. No case is really exactly the same as one that came before. We are used to partial matches when we use an old case to help with a new one. What we are not used to is a discussion of why one match was correct and why another was less helpful. Making case matching a conscious process helps us understand something that we normally do without much conscious thought. People need to learn to rely on partial matches and they need to know how to determine which partial match is most likely. I have referred to this process as case-based reasoning in many prior publications.[4] But I have not spoken about how to teach case-based reasoning. This is where post hoc discussion is very important. An example of such a discussion can be found in a book written by Harvard government professors[5] on the failure of President Ford to choose the right cases to reason from in a crisis. Usually this kind of analysis is done as kind of an afterthought. However, teaching people to do it actually is critical to teaching people to predict properly.

How do we teach prediction when there is no script and there are no seemingly relevant prior cases? In some sense we can't. We can teach people how to go about trying to make predictions. This is actually what science is about. Scientists create theories that make predictions, which they then try to verify with evidence. This process—hypotheses verified by evidence—can be taught in the sense that it is a way of thinking that can be practiced in various venues. It is reasonable to start teaching children to think in this way about the world around them. As for adults, teaching scientific reasoning in the context of corporate training is probably a less than optimal place to start. People in corporations need to be able to reason from evidence and to understand what data would confirm or deny the value of actions they have taken for the benefit of the company. This, of course, is scientific reasoning. But, unfortunately, the people who go into the business world tend to have never practiced scientific reasoning in their educational careers because they weren't interested in science. But they must be interested in predicting well in order to succeed in business.

HOW TO TEACH MODELING

Building a model of a process is very difficult for a child to do and not so easy for an adult to do either. When you teach computer science, you learn this quickly enough. Computer programs are models of processes. People try to write computer programs by creating diagrams that model what happens first and then what happens next, and so on. These models are almost never right the first time.

Programmers learn to debug their programs, which means they continue to try to get their model to be accurate. But most people cannot do this very easily, and it is a very important skill. Knowing how to raise money is important if one wants to start a business, for example. The money-raising process can be understood, but one has to examine it and go through it.

This is just as true of ordering in a restaurant. Children may seem to know about ordering in a restaurant, but they may not understand money or service or having a job exactly and thus may have an erroneous model of the process. Why does the waitress bring food, is a complex question for a 5-year-old, but also an important one. Building models of how and why things work as they do, is significant for children to learn to do.

The way to do this is to look at processes that children engage in during the course of their daily lives and have them first explain how and why the processes work and then try to improve upon them. They could carefully examine the operations of the school cafeteria, for example. Of course, this has to be done in line with the interests that the children actually have. The idea is building the model, not telling them what models they have to build. Every child has an interest—animals, sports, family, cars, dinosaurs, whatever. Children need to learn to model the processes that interest them in order to better understand them and to make them better. Children will learn about the modeling process from working on a car engine, for example, if they are taught to think about what is going on in a deep way rather than just learning a set of facts about how the car runs. This is true in any area of interest, from medicine to government to science.

Adults have a difficult time with models at work, as citizens, at home, and so on. They don't always know how things really work. To get people to be better at understanding the processes that they engage in daily life, they need to be able to model them. This ability has to be taught and practiced early.

Of course, kids have been building models of actual objects for a long time. Using a kit to build a model airplane is fun but it doesn't teach you much about how planes fly. More detailed models of physical objects are very helpful.

Building a medieval castle, for example, sounds like fun to me, and there are things to be learned from doing this, of course. It is a good activity for little kids, but modeling involves social processes as well. Kids need to understand how the world works, so it isn't the castle itself that is so important but perhaps a model of the society around the castle, and the need for the castle, that would matter in this instance.

HOW TO TEACH EXPERIMENTATION

Everyone experiments all the time. We eat foods that we hope won't make us fat or might make us healthy. We take drugs that are supposed to help us, and maybe they do maybe they don't. We try out relationships that may or may not work. We experiment with jobs, hobbies, homes, cars, toys, games, lifestyles, behaviors, hairdos. . . . The list is seemingly infinite.

We may not see ourselves as experimenting when we try out something new. We often experiment ineffectively. Learning to experiment in a reasonable way is yet again something that can be done only through experience. But, in this case, there really is an experimental process to be learned. It can be taught early on by finding simple experiments that small children really are interested in doing—they do not all have to do the same ones since it doesn't matter what they do. They can learn to attempt to control the variables and see what happens in a variety of circumstances. This is, again, the scientific method, but the issue is really not teaching science so much as it is teaching a scientific approach to gathering useful knowledge. What constitutes evidence and how to draw conclusions are the kinds of things that a teacher can help with. Here again, a case base is acquired and relied on throughout this process. The discussion of findings so that they can be mentally indexed is a very important part of the process.

But how do we find out what is true? Ask any 5-year-old this question and the answer is not very likely to be, We run an experiment. Ask mommy, is more likely or, Ask the teacher, if the kid is in school.

But, testing hypotheses is a critical part of learning to think. Of course, one has to have a hypothesis first. Children are rarely asked for their hypotheses about things. This is not exactly odd because although children do have them, it is a weird kind of discussion to have with a 5-year-old. Nevertheless, it is important to do. Teaching children to form and test hypotheses is as simple as asking them to do it. But, here again, asking them to do it must be done within the context of something they really care about. There have been many attempts over the course of educational history to teach kids science by having them run experiments; sometimes they are asked simply to replicate old experiments and sometimes they are asked to try new ideas out and figure things out for themselves. While the latter is most certainly preferable, these experiments tend to be about testing water quality, or nutrients in the soil, subjects that are not exactly on the mind of a 5-year-old.

What is on the mind of a 5-year-old? He might be wondering about how to deal with his baby sister. Or he might be wondering how best to throw a rock in order to hit the cat. For many of these things, hypotheses can be formed, discussions about what makes a good hypothesis can be had, and ideas for testing out hypotheses can be sought. Maybe these would just be thought experiments (as in the case of hitting the cat), but thought experiments are important also. Knowing what would confirm or deny a hypothesis is important. Finding out what kids want to get better at is part of the issue here. If they want to learn to hit a baseball, having a theory about what makes a good swing and what makes a bad one may matter to them. The subject matter doesn't matter at all really, just the thinking and the experimentation.

This suggests that the real way to teach experimentation and the other subjects we have discussed here is to group kids not by age but by interests. So, if a child wants to think about dogs all day, group him with a set of other dog lovers and start coming up with hypotheses about dogs' behavior, needs, commands that they might learn, training, breeding, and so on. It just doesn't matter what the subject is at this stage.

Suggestions for kids' science experiments are everywhere. Here is a typical one:

Gravity

The Earth tries to pull everything down toward its center. This pull is called the force of gravity (the invisible force). When you lift things up, you have to pull against gravity. If you drop a pencil, gravity pulls it to Earth. If you rest its midpoint on your finger, gravity will pull down equally on both sides of the pencil and it will balance in the air.

Here is another:

Sound and Noise

Have one person fill each of the plastic eggs with a different item. Put some rice in one, some dried beans in another, and so on. Keep track of what you put in each egg by writing numbers on the eggs. Have a different person try to see if he can figure out what is inside each egg by shaking and listening to the sound generated. After he takes a first guess, show him the list of what items are in each egg and have him guess again. See if he changes his mind about some of the previous guesses. Now open the eggs and see how close the guesses were to what was actually inside each egg.

Now, let's make a musical instrument called a kazoo. Cut a small square of wax paper about 1 inch larger than the end of the cardboard tube. After doing that, wrap the wax paper over one of the ends of the tube and put a rubber band over the paper to hold it in place. Now, put the open end of your kazoo up to your mouth and hum a tune into it. Notice how the kazoo buzzes and vibrates to amplify (make louder) the sound of your voice.

Of course, this is not exactly what I have in mind when I suggest focusing school on experimentation. Say the word *experiment* and the word *science* usually follows right away. This is unfortunate because most kids won't become scientists any time soon. Also, most kids already know what they are being asked to "experiment" about. They know the pencil falls and they know you can make noise by blowing through things. They may not understand how all this works, but they won't understand much more after doing these so-called "experiments."

Experiments in the larger sense are about attempts to find out what is true about things you are uncertain about. The issue is how to do that when you are wondering about something. To do this we need to constantly deal with what kids are worrying about and ask them to determine how they can find out what is true. This is experimentation that can be helped by teachers. It needs to be individually focused, however. You can't have a class worry collectively about any one thing. Each kid has his own concerns.

HOW TO TEACH EVALUATION

For an issue that is so important to so many people, it is astonishing how difficult this seems to be. Just say no to drugs campaigns don't work and people wonder why. Abstinence campaigns don't work and people wonder why. It is not all that mysterious. You can't teach evaluation verbally. Since children naturally copy their parents, it is not that complicated to figure out where children acquire their initial values. And, since values are not typically stated (my father never said liquor at 5 p.m. is a good thing), it certainly isn't through lectures that we learn values. I learned to drink at 5 p.m. from my father. He wasn't trying to teach me that. I learned to gamble from my father. He wasn't trying to teach me that either. I learned to be argumentative from my father. He wasn't trying to teach that. I did not learn algebra from my father. That, he was trying to teach me.

My son wanted to grow up and sip Pepsi. He told me this constantly as he was growing up. It did not matter that I hadn't drunk Pepsi for 10 years at the point when he was saying that. He was impressed that I had done this when he was 3 and he was frustrated that I didn't allow him to drink it. Presto, another family value is learned.

Children learn the family values that their family actually has. Teenage mothers who warn against getting pregnant at a young age may say that in words, but their actions say that their kid is alive and well and it all worked out.

So, it follows that we don't have to consciously teach values because we teach them without saying a word. Values are held subconsciously and learned subconsciously. We can only hope that we have set a good example. That having been said, there will still be those who ask how we can teach values. You can't expect that "you can't," will work as an answer.

I mentioned in Chapter 3 that there are lots of things that you can't teach. I mentioned honesty as an example. Honesty is, of course, a value. Now let's ask whether you can teach people to be more honest than they are naturally inclined to be. The answer is that to do this, you have to turn a subconscious process into a conscious one. You would need to provide case after case and experience after experience to a student that all led to the conclusion that honesty simply works out better in the long run. This is, of course, what abstinence and *say no to drugs* campaigns endeavor to do. They want to argue kids into believing that things they think are fun, are bad. But how can we make that argument? The argument we can make is that these things aren't as much fun as you think, so try them and see for yourself—but that kind of ruins the basic premise about not doing them in the first place. So, in principle there is no way to argue kids into not doing what looks like fun to them and what doesn't seem to have hurt anyone very much. The idea of showing pain is big in values campaigns. Campaigns against drunk driving like to show students dead drivers and awful car crashes. But they miss the real point. Have the students seen their parents drink and drive or friends drink and drive? Are they dead? If not, these campaigns will have little impact since values are subconsciously held.

There is a way to teach these things but it isn't easy. Imagine that you wanted to teach teenagers not to drive drunk. You could create a simulation of drunkenness that asked students to drive drunk while not being able to hold their heads steady, blacking out from time to time, and seeing very badly. In other words, instilling a new emotion into the mix can alter values. Make people afraid of something they want to do and that fear will manifest itself when it is time to do it. Emotions can be induced into subconscious processes and decision-making through experience. Emotions can change values.

There is a sense in which appreciation cannot be taught. You like it or you don't. I have two grandsons. The 5-year-old (my daughter's child) has announced that he doesn't want to have anything to do with a ball. The 3-year-old (my son's child) goes wild with excitement when he sees ballgames being played and responds excitedly when balls are given to him. What is the difference and how did this happen? The difference is obvious: One appreciates the art of it and one doesn't. How this happened is less clear, but the parenting is very different with respect to balls in each house. There are other, biological differences as well. The 3-year-old has much taller parents and is already the same size as the 5-year-old. He is much more physical as well.

So, the question is, Could we teach the 5-year-old to love balls and ballgames, and could we teach the 3-year-old to hate balls and ballgames? The answer to this is obvious. We could do this. It might be hard but people are, unfortunately, quite good at negative reinforcement, so it is possible to make people change their attitudes by using it as a method.

Is there a way to teach the positive? Can we get someone to appreciate a work of art who does not respond immediately to works of art? Can we get someone to appreciate classical music who does not have any interest in it?

This is, of course, what many art history or music appreciation courses endeavor to do. Their methodology is always the same:

repeated exposure and analysis. It always involves a lot of talking. And therein lies the problem. Since appreciation and enjoyment are subconscious processes, it stands to reason that these processes are best addressed by a methodology that is less conscious. Telling me why I should like something is not likely to do much more than teach me how to talk about something as if I liked it. I can point out the finer points of baseball to you, but if you don't care, I won't be able to get you to go to the next baseball game.

On the other hand, of course, you certainly won't like baseball if you have never seen it played. Exposure is the key to teaching subconscious processes. Add to that an enjoyable atmosphere surrounding the experience, especially if it is early on in one's life, associated with the artistry you want to teach, and it is likely that the learner will learn to like whatever he is being exposed to. So, evaluation, which starts out as a subconscious process, must be taught by enabling copying and repeated practice, but cannot easily be taught verbally.

HOW TO TEACH DIAGNOSIS

Diagnosis is the same and it is different. Many different people do diagnosis under many different circumstances. But, the process is always the same. So it seems normal to ask why an expert in doing diagnosis in one area cannot do diagnosis nearly as well in another area of knowledge. Why can't a doctor fix his own car? Why can't a detective figure out why a business is failing? It is all diagnosis after all.

Diagnosis is best taught early on but it can be taught at any age. In the end, it is just about knowing what counts as evidence and how to create and rule out hypotheses. The general process of gathering evidence and testing hypotheses is the same no matter what you are doing. This is true in principle, of course, not in actual fact. In reality, doctors cannot rule out hypotheses by tests that might harm the patient. Businesspeople cannot rule out hypotheses by running control businesses that may lose money while others make money. Detectives cannot spoil a crime scene by altering the evidence. Mechanics cannot try something that might make things worse. Investors cannot control world events that might make a seemingly correct hypothesis still not work out all that well.

To teach diagnosis, simple problems can be worked on that lead to more complex problems. What is being taught, apart from the process itself, is the knowledge that underlies the hypothesis and understanding what constitutes evidence and the consequences of evidence. This knowledge is very domain specific and is the reason that doctors don't necessarily make good car mechanics, and vice versa. This knowledge can be acquired only through practice and experience and can be acquired only consciously. Diagnosis is thus a conscious process that is very knowledge dependent. There is no seat-of-the-pants diagnosis, namely, diagnosis that is seemingly subconscious, although it may well seem that way. Having an intuition is usually just the result of having a great deal of experience, so much so that hypotheses just jump out at you because similar cases are so easily recognizable to an expert. Someone who is good at diagnosis would be good at diagnosis in any domain of knowledge if they knew how to gather and interpret evidence in that domain.

Diagnosis is clearly very difficult to learn. Most people are rather bad at it outside of their own areas of interest. Even inside their knowledge base they can be sloppy in the reasoning and leap to wrong conclusions. This is true of all analytic skills. It is possible to never learn to do them well.

HOW TO TEACH PLANNING

Planning is extremely important and typical of an analytic cognitive process; it is something that some people simply never learn to do well. Teaching planning must be focused around the assembly of a case base. Planning is taught in many domains of knowledge and is almost always taught wrong. The classic error is to teach the theory of planning, means–ends analysis, a theory of urban planning, spatial planning, military planning, and logic-based artificial intelligence planning. Such courses all make the same mistake. Course designers think people use theories when, in fact, when people plan, they simply try to adapt old plans that have worked before to new situations. Often people don't plan at all. They simply assume that a set of actions they intend to perform will work to achieve an expected goal.

Teaching planning is therefore a tedious process that is best begun in childhood. It involves making plans, seeing how they play out, and performing an analysis of what went wrong. Often people are not even aware that they have made a plan, and are simply frustrated when things go wrong. They almost never perform an after-action review (as the military calls the analysis process that takes place after a plan has been implemented).

Teaching planning means teaching about goals, how they typically are achieved, what obstacles might be encountered, and how to deal with them. The principles of planning are the same no matter what domain you are in, so children can learn to plan birthday parties, hikes, class trips, how to deal with their problems, how to treat their little sister, how to get along with their parents, and so on. This process can be learned by copying, seeing how others deal with these things, adapting a plan that has worked before, and so on. A teacher who tries to teach planning from first principles is teaching something that is easily forgotten as well as teaching a process that doesn't occur that much in real life. Chefs adapt old recipes or parts of old recipes. Generals adapt old battle plans or parts of old battle plans. Computer programmers use code that has worked before. Planning without a prior plan in mind really is quite unusual and generally not a good idea.

Planning, like diagnosis, should be a basic part of all curricula in school at all ages. People make plans all the time. They plan their lunch, they plan their day, they plan their trips, they plan their errands, and, of course, they plan their lives. It is astonishing that we don't teach planning all the time in every aspect of life. But we don't because this doesn't seem very academic. Since it is not explicitly taught to children, it is reasonable to ask how we might best teach planning to adults. Corporations want to teach financial planning, resource planning, supply chain planning, creating business plans, creating marketing plans, and so on. Planning is, in fact, one of the major preoccupations of business, as well it should be. So, how do we teach it?

The problem here is that planning really works in only one way. It is relies on a case base. We plan by adapting old plans. That's how we do it. We store old plans and we retrieve them when we need them again; we change them so they apply to the new situation or change them so that this time they will work out when they failed before. But we always start with an old plan. New planners, those we are trying to teach how to plan, cannot help but do this, even if they do not have a relevant old plan to work from. They simply will choose the best plan they have, even though it might not be all that germane to the current situation. Proverbs—for example, to a man with a hammer, everything is a nail—don't come from nowhere.

Thus, when we teach planning, there is either a lot to undo, or we must start from the beginning. We can try to explain why each and every old plan is not really helpful in a new situation, or we can teach a series of plans that are relevant. In other words, if you are trying to teach people to write a business plan, you need to start with a lemonade stand and work up. If you are trying to teach financial planning, you need to start with a child's allowance and work up. If you want to teach battle planning, try a tug of war first. This is what should have occurred in childhood. If it didn't, it needs to be restarted that way for adults. We need to use, again and again, plans in different situations that are simple and begin to analyze why they fail. (And these plans must fail, at least in simulation, or no real learning will occur.)

Planning is very difficult. It must start simple and be practiced simply for a while or it never becomes second nature. Plans must fail, at least in simulation, because analysis of what went wrong is a critical part of planning. If you aren't analyzing what went wrong, you aren't learning to plan. Your case base will not end up having been indexed well enough to enable you to pick and choose appropriate plans in the future.

HOW TO TEACH CAUSATION

At the root of diagnosis and planning is causation. Detecting cause is an essential part of diagnosis, and anticipating cause is an important aspect of planning. Causation must be understood in order to do many things in this world. One needs to know what causes what. Science courses in school attempt to teach causation by having students memorize $F = ma$, or having them imitate chemistry experiments, or having them dissect a frog. While there is nothing wrong with any of that in principle, it really doesn't teach causation in a way that is particularly useful to a functioning adult.

While diagnosis and planning may not be recognized as critical skills by schools, causation is, although not under that word. Causation is understood as being what science is all about, and when schools endeavor to teach science, they are in fact trying to teach causation. This is true for social science as well. History is about causation, as is psychology. The fact that these subjects are not talked about in this way indicates something important about them.

Subject-based education makes the academic disciplines the center of what needs to be learned, when there is really something else at the base of learning. All human learning and all scientific inquiry is about causation; attempts to determine what causes what, and why, are what it means to be a scientist or an academic. Theories of causation, and tests to see whether those theories are true, are what it means to be a scientist.

The problem is that telling students that causation is part of science makes them think about physics formulas and fact memorization when the real issue in teaching causation is how to determine what causes what, rather than how to memorize what causes what. There are, of course, facts about causation that are worth knowing. It is nice to know that if you let go of something, it may fall, but it is not necessary to know that gravity is the issue in this. The world went on quite well for millions of years before Newton. People certainly understood before Newton that things would fall when you let go of them and nothing else was supporting them. Scientific explanations of causation are nice for scientists but not necessary for everyday humans. What everyday people need to know is how to determine what causes what in areas of their own interest. They can hear you tell them about causation—the stock market always goes down when a Democrat is elected president—but they need to be able to decide whether what you said is true and whether it is the election that causes the decline or something else.

Understanding about causation is much more a function of being able to figure out what caused what in any given instance than it is the memorization of facts about science. Of course, with known cases, as we have seen, being able to extrapolate from one case to another is a good way of determining what is likely to happen. There is no harm in knowing prior cases and great value in being able to use them. But, as always, cases are better learned from one's own experience than from being told about them.

Teaching causation, therefore, means teaching the process of determining what happened in any given situation. Since there is a great deal to learn about any domain of inquiry in order to determine causation, the main issue is how to know what the facts are and how to reason from them. This means that, yet again, it is the domain of knowledge that needs to be learned, and this entails constant practice in that domain. And, the methodology of determining causation needs to be learned. This, too, can depend on the particular domain of inquiry. Reasoning from all this takes practice as well. Determining cause is a critical cognitive process that underlies nearly all thinking.

HOW TO TEACH JUDGMENT

How do we get good at making a judgment? Judgments are a kind of prediction, of course. When a judge sentences a criminal, he is, in a sense, making a prediction about what will happen in the rest of this person's life. But he also is making a decision that is no way a prediction, but simply serves as punishment. Similarly, when we decide that a certain restaurant is our favorite, we are predicting something about how much we will enjoy future experiences, but we also are making a decision that may or may not matter to others, that is, a recommendation. Recommendations are also predictions, but they have a different feel. When a boss decides whom to promote, he is predicting something about future behavior but, again, the prediction isn't the key point. A judgment is a decision that has some import.

Nevertheless, as different as judgments and predictions may or may not be, the process of teaching them is identical. Good judgment is learned by making judgments and analyzing the results or truth of those judgments as more information becomes available. After a judgment is made it too becomes one of one's cases and stories. Cases about judgment can be learned only by making simple judgments and getting smarter about the process over time on the basis of experience.

Judgments can be made in two ways that matter here. Either someone can decide to do one thing versus another thing based on ethical, moral, avaricious, or emotional grounds, or for many other reasons. Judgments aren't so different from decisions in this aspect. Teaching someone to make a judgment of this sort, between A and B, can be done by putting students in situations in which such judgments need to be made and then going over with them how they decided and what they may have left out of their thinking.

A different kind of judgment is made when one judges the behavior of others. Judges do this, of course, as do compliance officers in companies, and teachers with respect to student mistakes.

Children normally make judgments about the behavior of their parents and friends as well. In all these cases, judgment is best taught by having a student watch the behavior of others, keeping himself out of the issue and seeing what factors motivated and determined the behavior of the actors. It is a lot easier to teach proper behavior when it is not one's own behavior that is being judged. One can learn to act by judging how others act.

So, children make judgments all the time. Typically those judgments reflect the values that they have been taught at home. Children decide what is good and what is bad mostly based on what they have been told. No child discovers for himself that George Washington was an admirable man. No child decides on his own that the United States is the best country in the world. These things are taught by parents and by schools. School, to the extent that it serves as a place of indoctrination, has always succeeded at producing citizens who believe what they are taught to believe at a young age. There obviously is a great deal of sentiment for keeping indoctrination as a key part of education, but teaching judgment means allowing children to come to conclusions based on their own experience and not merely what they were told.

Learning to make judgments is a process of deciding for oneself what is true, which is, of course, not so easy. This should be the role of school but it usually isn't. School wants to teach us the truth when, in fact, truth is best discovered, again, from experience.

How would one discover the "best country in the world," if that is a meaningful idea, or whether George Washington was all he was cracked up to be? Obviously, travel helps teach one about countries. Kids can learn about countries by simulated travel in the modern era. But the point wouldn't be so much to teach them that they make good cheese in France, which is the kind of thing school does today, but to think about what makes France different from the United States. Similarly, we can read and learn some facts about George Washington, and these are indeed taught to children in primary school. I do not believe that children are equipped at a young age to determine for themselves whether Washington was a good man. Perhaps that would be a worthwhile assignment in high school, as long as students were interested in the question and were allowed to come to any conclusion that they could reasonably defend. But children of 5 or 6 can understand what a hero is and what leadership is, and they can determine for them-selves who they know or have seen who is good at both. Again, real experiences and discussions are how one learns to think about this, but it must be done in an environment of possible truths, not prede-termined truths. One doesn't create a nation of people who can think by telling them what they should think. Kids know who is the leader among them. They should learn to discuss what it is about their leader that makes them want to follow. This is a difficult discussion to have with a 6-year-old, but it gets easier with age.

Once again, asking kids to make judgments isn't that unusual. Here is a remark from a parenting book that I happened upon:

> When adults praise their kids for smart judgments, the kids glow. But here's the clincher: kids earn more and more freedom and independence when parents trust their judgments more and more.[6]

The issue here is, yet again, not whether kids make judgments, but whether they are taught, as a central part of what they study, how to make judgments.

The cognitive processes depend on reasoning from evidence in a way that makes sense. This is not something people are naturally good at. They often exhibit faulty reasoning. Practicing reasoning means practicing within particular domains of knowledge. Reasoning is the same process no matter what you are reasoning about, but we don't reason about nothing. Learning the actual facts is important, but it is the idea that this is important that has sent the school systems on the wrong path. Academics study the facts, as well they should, but they also teach the facts, which is a grievous error. How to determine the facts and how to determine their effects on a situation is what the processes of diagnosis, planning, and causation are all about.

HOW TO TEACH INFLUENCE

This is yet another childhood skill. Children learn how to influence their parents and their siblings and their friends very early on. Of course, they may not learn these things in a good way. They might learn that temper tantrums or bullying works very well.

Teaching people how to influence people involves putting them in situations where it is possible to influence people and seeing how it goes. There is nothing to learn exactly. We try behaviors and see what works. What works for one person may not work for another. One way or another, we learn how to get what we want, or we learn to hang out with people who will respond to our needs. This is basically a subconscious process. We are so busy working on this at a very young age that we may not have any idea what it is we know or how to improve what we do. Of course, there is a conscious part as well. Someone can tell us that we will catch more flies with honey than with vinegar, and we can, if we think about it, adjust our behavior. But aphorisms about what works and what doesn't work aren't always correct and are highly idiosyncratic. Although there are books about how to win friends and influence people, the reality is that, apart from adopting a phony personality, people are who they are, more or less.

But this does not mean they can't be taught what works. It usually does mean that they can be taught what works as a result of their own experience. And, they can be taught what doesn't work as a result of their own experience. But this isn't at all easy. If it were, psychiatrists would not be able to make a living. You can tell a person to change his behavior, you can even tell him exactly what to do when, but he is likely not going to be able to do what you say.

The way influence is taught currently is probably the way it has to be taught, then, by use of mentors who look at your behavior and talk you through why you do what you do. This same mentoring method can be used in corporate settings. Simulations may not be so effective because while we may know and be able to say the right answer, this doesn't mean that we can execute the desired behavior in reality.

HOW TO TEACH TEAMWORK

Teamwork is learned by working in teams. It is a mixed process because, here again, we behave in ways that are not so conscious but we can make conscious changes. Leaders learn to manage teams by thinking about what works and what doesn't. Quarterbacks must learn to manage their teammates. If they don't, it really doesn't matter how well they can throw the ball. Team members have to want to work hard for the leader, and the leader has to know how to motivate each team member. People are different so what works for one may not work for another. A leader learns to figure out who is who and what works for each member of the team. The conscious part of this is about learning who needs what from the leader in order for the leader to get the most out of each individual so that the team's goals are achieved. The subconscious part is about interacting with others, which is rarely conscious behavior. We get smarter through experience. If our team wins because we functioned well as a team, we learn to repeat the behaviors that worked. If we win because our team was simply much bigger than the other team, then we probably won't learn much about teamwork.

Teamwork can be taught only by examining how a team functions and attempting to make conscious the subconscious behavior that is not working. Thinking about what we have done that may not have been helpful to the team, and making sure that team members' goals are aligned, is pretty much the only way we can learn to improve our behavior.

HOW TO TEACH NEGOTIATION

My daughter was a little over 2 when we moved back to the United States from Switzerland. The enormity of U.S. toy stores overwhelmed her and it seemed that she wound up crying every time we entered one. She wanted everything. So I had what I thought was a clever idea. I told her that she could have two toys of her choice but that if she cried she couldn't get any at all. We talked about it and it was clear that she had understood what I said. She ran around the toy store and ended up selecting three toys. I told her one would have to go back—that our agreement was two. She started crying hysterically. I then said she had to put them all back as she had violated our no crying agreement. All of sudden, she sucked up all her tears and said in a breathless voice: I'm not crying now. I said that we would compromise on one toy.

That was possibly her first lesson in negotiating. I say possibly because kids and parents negotiate all the time. She and I are still negotiating. Now it is about when she will come to visit or when she will send her son down to visit or a range of other family issues.

Negotiation is so important that it is nearly absurd to ask how we teach negotiation. We can learn it by copying, of course, which I did when I watched my father get a good price on a used car I was buying that I was ready to pay much more for. But really we negotiate with our wives and children and friends and co-workers all the time.

It is possible to teach negotiation, of course. My team once built a course on negotiation, working with a Harvard Law professor[7] who taught negotiation. The course worked by having people negotiate. The situations were artificial so there is some question as to how valuable lessons can be learned from negotiating when nothing important (except ego) depends on it. What I found most interesting about that course were the stories that the expert told from his life as a professional negotiator. I can't say that I was ever able to personally make use of the lessons that those stories taught, but other people's experiences are interesting to think about. In the end, what we really know about negotiation is what has worked well for us in the course of our lives when we were negotiating. Coaching can help, of course, which implies that the best way to teach negotiation would be with a mentor watching you do it for real and offering tips. Psychologists perform this service in couples counseling, and presumably real estate agents perform this service for homebuyers and sellers. Just-in-time advice is always helpful.

HOW TO TEACH DESCRIBING

There is a famous quote: "I apologize that this letter is so long—I lacked the time to make it short."[8] As long as people have been talking, they have had to learn to talk well. When they learned to write, they had to learn to write well. Communication is a very big part of living in a society and those who communicate well gain all kinds of advantages. It is difficult to attain public office without speaking well, or to become an important academic without writing well, or to make sales or convince anyone of anything without making your case well.

This takes practice and coaching, and there is no substitute for either. One also has to have something to say, so this means one has to have had experiences to talk and write about. Further, it helps if one is writing about something that one is passionate about. Asking kids to write about their summer vacations doesn't necessarily make them into good writers. Asking kids to give speeches about George Washington fails for reasons of lack of passion. People need to learn to describe well what is most important to them. And, they must be doing this in every task they undertake. They must talk about and write about what they do until the description process becomes second nature to them. So, describing cannot be taught in and of itself. It must be part and parcel of other events students undertake. Writing classes make no sense, therefore. They exist because of the subject-based divisions in school. Writing and speaking must be part of everything that is going on.

SUMMARY

Proficiency at all the cognitive processes depends on discovery and being able to extrapolate from one's experience about what has been discovered. These processes depend strongly on prior cases, and prior cases are best learned slowly in childhood. They also depend on an analysis of those cases, which is best done with help from a teacher. Discussion, reflection, and analysis of prior cases make one better able to deal with new cases. New cases must be compared with old ones in a way that helps one reason better from them. This comparison is the basis of teaching analytic cognitive processes. Learning cognitive processes means having prior experiences with events that are similar to current events and being able to extrapolate from them. When we go to a doctor, we want one who has seen our problem, and described it to others, many times before. Only then can we detect the nuances of difference that will determine an effective course of action.

Teaching cognitive processes means providing students with experiences, hopefully each one more complex than the one before, and helping students discuss those experiences and compare one with another. Knowledge is experience, but it is experience that has been analyzed so that it can be retrieved again just in time as needed. This will happen only if we have thought about what we have experienced.

A teacher's job, therefore, is to help provide the experiences and to help the student reflect upon the significance of those experiences. Good parents do this naturally. Good teachers would do it naturally as well, if they were allowed to do so. Helping someone see the world in a new way is pretty much what good teaching is all about.

CHAPTER 10

Defining Intelligence

All our knowledge begins with the senses, proceeds then to the understanding, and ends with reason. There is nothing higher than reason.

—Immanuel Kant

What is school for? A common answer is, to make people more knowledgeable. Another is, to socialize them and prepare them for living with others. Another is, to make them ready for work. (This last one seems almost laughable because it is clearly untrue in the modern world, but people do seem to still believe it.) Another is, to prepare them for more school. (People take this one very seriously.) My answer is: School should make people more intelligent.

Really? Can we make people more intelligent? There are those who would argue, and I am quite sure they are right, that intelligence is genetic: It can't be altered by school, one way or the other.

Nevertheless, I think that school should make students more intelligent.

How can I believe both things?

It all depends on how you define intelligence. Let's think about intelligence the way ordinary people define it when they say that someone seems dumb or that someone seems to be very smart. There is a lot to be learned by considering seriously the folk view of intelligence as opposed to the classical school/testing view.

In the 2007 Miss Teen USA contest, Miss South Carolina responded to this question:

"Recent polls have shown that a fifth of Americans can't locate the United States on a world map. Why do you think this is?"

In this way:

> "I personally believe, that U.S. Americans, are unable to do so,
> because uh, some, people out there, in our nation don't have
> maps, and uh . . . I believe that our education like such as in
> South Africa, and the Iraq, everywhere like such as . . . and, I
> believe they should uh, our education over here, in the U.S.
> should help the U.S. or should help South Africa, and should
> help the Iraq and Asian countries so we will be able to build up
> our future, for us."

Millions of Americans upon hearing this interview, which was re-
played on every television outlet, thought this response was both very
funny and an indication of how stupid Miss South Carolina was. Most
adults feel that they know what intelligence looks like and that they
know what stupidity looks like. Everyone agreed about the absurdity
of this response. It was, after all, incoherent, and this was obvious to
anybody.

Miss South Carolina was given another chance to answer the
question on the *Today Show* on NBC, some days later. Here is a
description of what happened from the MSNBC website:

> She explained Tuesday that she was so overwhelmed by the
> moment she barely heard any of the question.
>
> "Everything did come at me at once," she said. "And I made
> a mistake—everybody makes a mistake—I'm human. Right when
> the question was asked of me, I was in shock . . . I would love to
> re-answer that question."
>
> Curry [of the Today show] obliged, reading the entire
> question as it had been asked during the pageant. This time,
> Upton [Miss South Carolina] was ready.
>
> "Personally, my friends and I, we know exactly where the
> United States is on a map," she said. "I don't know anyone else
> who doesn't. If the statistics are correct, I believe there should
> be more emphasis on geography in our education so people will
> learn how to read maps better."
>
> She came back later in the show to deliver a flawless
> explanation of lunar eclipses.
>
> Held up on the Internet as the quintessential dumb blonde,
> Upton was an honor student in high school.

The premise here is that she isn't actually stupid but was just con-fused by the moment and that she is intelligent because she is on the honor roll at school, can explain lunar eclipses, and could answer the original question coherently, given sufficient time to do it (and maybe with some help).

The media, for reasons of their own, decided to make this a feel-good story and get people to feel better about Miss South Carolina. She has continued to work in the media in various ways since the original interview.

I am not concerned here with Miss South Carolina's intelligence, but with what it means to be seen as being intelligent. My premise is that while native intelligence is certainly genetic, the perception of intelligence and what might be described as intelligent behavior can be altered. (Perhaps this seems as incoherent a position as Miss South Carolina's position on education.)

The curious thing about her second response is that it doesn't answer the original question at all. The question was about why she thought Americans were ignorant about geography, and she respond-ed by saying that they weren't but that maybe there should be more education about reading maps, which in no way addresses the ques-tion about why Americans can't locate the United States on a map.

So her answer is still awful even after she was given time to work on it. It is simply unintelligent.

The question is: Could we make Miss South Carolina more intel-ligent somehow? Clearly school hasn't done it. (She was an honor student!) How might one do it?

Of course, we really aren't concerned with Miss South Carolina in particular. Consider the following interviews conducted at a Sarah Palin book signing in November 2009, in Columbus, Ohio. The interviewees were all in line waiting to meet Sarah Palin and to buy her book:

> Interviewer: Tell us why you are here today.
> Older woman: She stands for what America is.
> Interviewer: What do you mean by that?
> Older woman: Freedom, liberty, right to speak . . .
> Interviewer: What are the particular issues you would like to see her bring to office?
> Older woman: Oh, geez, help me out here, guys.
> Second woman: Fairness. Realness.

So we have a Palin supporter who has no idea why she supports Palin and asks for help. The "helper" says fairness and realness, which apart from being ungrammatical is also nonsense. Neither supporter seems to know much about Palin, but they are eager to meet her and they believe in her. (This is not a comment about Sarah Palin, at least not by me. Supporters of most political candidates have difficulty explaining why they like whomever they like. Or, alternatively, they can explain it and those explanations leave you wondering.)

I will never forget attending a JFK campaign visit to Brooklyn when I was 14. The woman next to me exclaimed that *she would vote for JFK because he was so gorgeous.* I was appalled. I knew the woman. She was not a deep thinker, but, really–people vote for someone because of their looks? Yes, people do, political scientists have pointed this out consistently.

Is this intelligent behavior? Of course not.

The question is: Can we do something about it? Is this an aspect of intelligence that is not genetic and that therefore can be changed?

If you know and believe that what you have just said makes no sense, you can try to learn how to make sense. Do these people know that are they are not making sense? Here is another person from that same Columbus event:

> Young man in Ohio State jacket: She's the epitome of
> conservativeness and I'm telling you if the Republican Party
> doesn't back her, it doesn't matter because she's going to get
> the presidency.
> Interviewer: What would you like to see her do with foreign
> policy?
> Young man in Ohio State jacket: To be honest with you I don't
> know anything about her foreign policy.
> Interviewer: What are some of the problems you have with cap
> and trade proposed by Democrats in office?
> Young man in Ohio State jacket: You want to give away your own
> money, it's fine, but don't tell me to give away my money. It's
> socialism.
> Young man in Ohio State jacket: The state that she did govern
> was right across the street from Russia. You know so I'm not
> saying that she ever had to deal with Russia but I'm sure she

had boundary issues she had to deal with. We have boundary issues right now with Mexico now.

This Palin supporter is also incoherent but incoherent in a different way. He doesn't know much, and he knows he doesn't know much. But he has beliefs and he believes in his beliefs. He has beliefs about socialism (that it is bad, and that President Obama thinks it is good) that are based on no real knowledge. He has beliefs about foreign policy and what it means to have foreign policy experience that are based on nonsense. And he has made up some beliefs about "boundaries."

What does this tell us? It tells us that at some point, maybe not now because he is too set in his own beliefs, someone could have taught him about socialism or "boundaries" or what it means to have foreign policy experience. But it should be clear that this is exactly the kind of education that we have been trying to do in our schools forever. You can talk about socialism in school, but that doesn't mean that your average person learns much from what is said there.

There is a wonderful movie called *Ferris Bueller's Day Off* that reveals a great deal about education. I often use a clip from that movie, when I give speeches on education or training, wherein the teacher drones on about the Smoot Hawley tariff and George Bush's view of Reagan's voodoo economics (as stated in the 1980 primaries) while the students doze off. At a different point in the same movie, the lead character blows off a European history test, saying:

> It's on European socialism. I mean, really! What's the point? I'm not European . . . I don't plan on being European. So who gives a crap if they're socialists? They could be fascist anarchists. . . . It still wouldn't change the fact that I don't own a car!

They do teach about socialism in school, but no one is listening. If we can't produce reasonably intelligent voters in our schools, then we aren't doing much.

Here is another Columbus Palin fan:

> Interviewer: What do you think she would bring in terms of policy in office?

Young woman: Good judgment.
Interviewer: Any specifics?
Young woman: I think she would control the out-of-control
    spending.
Young woman: I think she would acknowledge the system of
    government in the United States rather than focus on the
    administration of czars.
Interviewer: Yeah, and what is your problem with czars?
Young woman: I'm an American and we don't have czars in
    America.

Here again, we have a juxtaposition of beliefs based on no actual evidence or reality. I don't know what this woman has heard about czars, but whatever it is, it misses the point. Could we teach this woman to be on point—to say meaningful things based on actual evidence? Not now, I fear, but it is my contention that we could have done so at some point in her life. School has failed her and she seems, to anyone listening, to be stupid. But she is not really stupid; she is just talking stupidly because she hasn't been challenged to behave in any other way.

Here is another:

Middle-aged woman: Governor of Alaska is the only one that has
    top security.
Interviewer: What does that mean?
Middle-aged woman: It means that if anything happens to our
    borders on that side, she's the first one in line for attack for
    there.

This person not only makes no sense, but she can't speak in an understandable way. Is that genetic? I doubt it. Intelligence, as it is popularly defined, includes the ability to produce coherent speech, which certainly can be enhanced through teaching, but apparently not by our schools as they currently exist.

Here is one last interview from that event:

Interviewer: What do you think of foreign policy—what would
    you like to see her do with foreign policy?
Man with cap: I don't know, I really don't have an answer—I
    don't know her well enough. I don't know what she knows or
    doesn't know. I don't know some stuff of what people ask me.

Interviewer: Some of the viewers think there's not enough oil.

Man with cap: We got us self-sufficient energy gas oil right under our feet. Why aren't we exploring more for it and drilling here instead of sending all that money overseas and exporting, I mean importing, all that oil back to America?

Interviewer: Do you hope she runs for president in 2012?

Man with cap: Yes, I do.

Interviewer: You will support her?

Man with cap: I sure would.

Interviewer: Do you think there will be any problems supporting her, knowing that you're unfamiliar with her foreign policy issues?

Man with cap: That wouldn't keep me from not voting for her.

There is a difference between ignorance and stupidity, just as there is a difference between knowledge and intelligence. It is a good guess that the "man with cap" above is both stupid and ignorant. The question is why?

One reason is that it is now acceptable in our society to be ignorant and stupid. Here is some of the famous ABC/Charles Gibson interview with Sarah Palin during the 2008 presidential campaign:

Gibson: Do you agree with the Bush doctrine?

Palin: In what respect, Charlie?

Gibson: The Bush—well, what do you—what do you interpret it to be?

Palin: His worldview.

Gibson: No, the Bush doctrine, enunciated September 2002, before the Iraq war.

Palin: I believe that what President Bush has attempted to do is rid this world of Islamic extremism, terrorists who are hellbent on destroying our nation. There have been blunders along the way, though. There have been mistakes made. And with new leadership, and that's the beauty of American elections, of course, and democracy, is with new leadership comes opportunity to do things better.

Gibson: The Bush doctrine, as I understand it, is that we have the right of anticipatory self-defense, that we have the right to a preemptive strike against any other country that we think is going to attack us. Do you agree with that?

Palin: Charlie, if there is legitimate and enough intelligence that tells us that a strike is imminent against American people, we have every right to defend our country. In fact, the president has the obligation, the duty to defend.

I suppose it is not a crime to not know the doctrine of the sitting president from your own party when you are running for vice president, but it does seem odd. But what is worse, is that after being told what that doctrine is, Palin is content to ramble on incoherently. Why doesn't this bother her? Clearly this is not a real issue because it doesn't bother her supporters either.

Here is some more from that interview:

Gibson: But this is not just reforming a government. This is also running a government on the huge international stage in a very dangerous world. When I asked John McCain about your national security credentials, he cited the fact that you have commanded the Alaskan National Guard and that Alaska is close to Russia. Are those sufficient credentials?

Palin: But it is about reform of government and it's about putting government back on the side of the people, and that has much to do with foreign policy and national security issues. Let me speak specifically about a credential that I do bring to this table, Charlie, and that's with the energy independence that I've been working on for these years as the governor of this state that produces nearly 20% of the U.S. domestic supply of energy, that I worked on as chairman of the Alaska Oil and Gas Conservation Commission, overseeing the oil and gas development in our state to produce more for the United States.

Gibson: I know. I'm just saying that national security is a whole lot more than energy.

Knowledge should matter for high government officials, but it doesn't matter precisely because the people who are listening have no knowledge either. Is Sarah Palin intelligent? There are plenty who would say that she is not. These include those who rank coherent thinking and the ability to create coherent explanations high on their list of what constitutes intelligence. But, it should be clear, that is not what generally is thought of as intelligence. IQ tests have been measuring intelligence for decades with questions like these:

> At the end of a banquet 10 people shake hands with each other. How many handshakes will there be in total?
>
> A. 100
> B. 20
> C. 45
> D. 50
> E. 90

> The day before the day before yesterday is three days after Saturday. What day is it today?
>
> A. Monday
> B. Tuesday
> C. Wednesday
> D. Thursday
> E. Friday

> Which number should come next in the series 1, 3, 6, 10, 15?
>
> A. 8
> B. 11
> C. 24
> D. 21
> E. 27

> Library is to book as book is to
>
> A. page
> B. copy
> C. binding
> D. cover

It is a reasonable guess that neither Palin nor her supporters would do really well on questions like these. But the real issue is why questions like these were chosen to be on IQ tests in the first place. Certainly our concept of intelligence, and how to measure it, depends on some vague sense of mathematical reasoning ability rather than real-life situation reasoning ability.

The schools make the same distinction. They do not seriously debate foreign policy in high school, but they do teach how to do number sequences. There might be those who would say that Palin and her supporters probably didn't do well on the math SAT either. But to me this is just a nonsensical way to look at intelligence. Plenty of smart people don't do well in, nor do they care about, math. But smart people do well in reasoning logically from evidence and in presenting a coherent argument for their beliefs. This is the essence of what it means to be smart and to be educated. We expect leaders to be coherent in what they say and to be able to justify their beliefs and actions. One can assume that those who are bad at number sequences present no problem for the country in any way, but being bad at detecting faulty reasoning has its consequences in a democracy.

Here is a bit from the Katie Couric interview with Sarah Palin that was shown on CBS during the 2008 campaign:

Couric: Why, in your view, is *Roe v. Wade* a bad decision?

Palin: I think it should be a states' issue not a federal government-mandated, mandating yes or no on such an important issue. I'm, in that sense, a federalist, where I believe that states should have more say in the laws of their lands and individual areas. Now, foundationally, also, though it's no secret that I'm pro-life, that I believe in a culture of life is very important for this country. Personally that's what I would like to see, um, further embraced by America.

Couric: Do you think there's an inherent right to privacy in the Constitution?

Palin: I do. Yeah, I do.

Couric: The cornerstone of *Roe v. Wade*.

Palin: I do. And I believe that individual states can best handle what the people within the different constituencies in the 50 states would like to see their will ushered in an issue like that.

Couric: What other Supreme Court decisions do you disagree with?

Palin: Well, let's see. There's, of course in the great history of America there have been rulings, that's never going to be absolute consensus by every American. And there are those issues, again, like *Roe v. Wade*, where I believe are best held on a state level and addressed there. So, you know, going through the history of America, there would be others but . . .

Couric: Can you think of any?

Palin: Well, I could think of . . . any again, that could be best dealt with on a more local level. Maybe I would take issue with. But, you know, as mayor, and then as governor and even as a vice president, if I'm so privileged to serve, wouldn't be in a position of changing those things but in supporting the law of the land as it reads today.

So little of what Palin says makes sense that this interview was seen as a national embarrassment, provoking multiple explanations for it from the Palin camp, none of which said: She is just stupid and ignorant.

Obviously that is what her detractors were thinking. But is it true? Is she stupid and ignorant? How can we find out? Look at this next piece of the Couric interview:

Couric: . . . people have questioned your readiness since that interview. And I'm curious to hear your reaction.

Palin: Well, not only am I ready but willing and able to serve as vice president with Senator McCain if Americans so bless us and privilege us with the opportunity of serving them, ready with my executive experience as a city mayor and manager, as a governor, as a commissioner, a regulator of oil and gas, not only with my résumé proving that readiness, but I think the important thing here is that John McCain and I, we share a vision for America that includes energy independence.

What could be clearer than the idea that she is simply out of her league and that it was a foolish idea to promote her as a possible vice president? Why cynical politicians decide this is OK to do is not my problem. The question I want to address is what makes one intelligent, apart from genetics.

Looking at what we have seen here, we can think about our 12 cognitive processes one more time. Which of them are critical to the everyday assessment of the intelligence of another person that most people do on a daily basis?

Let's start by eliminating some. Being able to evaluate something, or having a set of values you believe in, has very little to do with basic intelligence. The samples of stupidity that I cite above do not indicate that any of this ability—determining what is important—is missing in the people being interviewed.

Similarly, these people probably can influence one another, work in teams, and negotiate with one another to some extent. They may not be great at it, but we wouldn't characterize the ability to influence others well as a sign of intelligence. Many world leaders are very influential but not all of them are considered to be brilliant.

Similarly, the ability to be a good team player is no way considered to be a sign of intelligence. Some very bright people have difficulty working with others. These things are not signs of intelligence.

Modeling and experimentation ability aren't really important when we talk about intelligence. Experimentation is something scientists do. Children and chefs and nonscientists do it as well, of course. But we wouldn't criticize these interviewees if it turned out that they didn't know how to experiment. We certainly have no idea from these interviews whether they can experiment or not. We can guess that they cannot. We tend to think that experimentation is the province of brilliant people, but would we say that someone is unintelligent because they don't know how to conduct a real experiment? Or, that a chef is brilliant because he takes risks with food? (We may say that he is a brilliant chef, but that doesn't mean we think he is brilliant.) Experimentation has a lot to do with innovation, which is certainly related to intelligence, but, again, it really is not what we think about when we hear interviews and think that the people being interviewed are stupid.

Similarly, we don't know whether these folks can effectively create a model of the world. It seems a good guess that they cannot, but, yet again, this lies more within the province of science and very intelligent thinking than within our everyday definition of intelligence. Some very smart people have weird models of the world or no model of certain aspects of the world.

We do not think that the interviewees are stupid because they don't conduct experiments or create elaborate world models.

But a different story emerges when we look at the rest of the cognitive processes. Which of the remaining processes are clearly missing in the answers supplied by the interviewees above?

Obviously these people don't speak particularly well.

Being able to aptly describe your views, or describe a situation you have been in, or a thought you have had, is a hallmark of intelligence.

We judge people's intelligence, at least in part, by how well they speak.

Does the ability to do diagnosis serve as a hallmark of intelligence?

Certainly doctors do diagnosis on a daily basis and doctors are highly respected in our society. Most people think that if you are a doctor, then you must be smart, but if you push on this belief, you find that what people actually think is that a doctor had to go to school for a really long time, learn of lot of complicated material, and then work really hard as an intern and then as a resident. People respect doctors and may well think that the doctor is the smartest person in their small town, but that is typically because she is likely the most educated person in that town. They easily may not consider her to have "common sense," which is one way that ordinary people describe their perception of intelligent behavior.

Diagnosis is done by plumbers, detectives, engineers, and beauty care professionals as well. Diagnosis is a very important cognitive process to learn. Learning to do it well often means the difference between success and failure on the job and personally. Can the interviewees do diagnosis? Miss South Carolina can.

She asserts that her friends can locate the United States on a map of the world. She can find contradictory evidence for the proposition presented to her, which is certainly part of diagnosis. The Palin interviewees have done diagnosis as well. They have determined what is wrong with the country. They may not have done much more than listen to someone on talk radio, but they came to a conclusion based on the evidence presented to them.

But they have done it badly. That is why they seem stupid.

Coming up with an accurate diagnosis requires intelligence. Everyone does diagnosis, but we seek counsel from those who do it better than others. *Diagnostic ability is a hallmark of intelligence.*

What about causation? Let's consider Miss South Carolina's revised remarks again:

> "Personally, my friends and I, we know exactly where the United States is on a map," she said. "I don't know anyone else who doesn't. If the statistics are correct, I believe there should be more emphasis on geography in our education so people will learn how to read maps better."

Miss South Carolina thinks "there should be more emphasis on geography in our education so people will learn to read maps better."

In many ways this remark is as dumb as her early remarks. Why do I think this?

Because it makes it clear that she hasn't a clue, and doesn't really care, about causation.

And, this is exactly the problem with Sarah Palin's remarks to Katie Couric as well:

> Couric: . . . people have questioned your readiness since that interview. And I'm curious to hear your reaction.
>
> Palin: Well, not only am I ready but willing and able to serve as vice president with Senator McCain if Americans so bless us and privilege us with the opportunity of serving them, ready with my executive experience as a city mayor and manager, as a governor, as a commissioner, a regulator of oil and gas, not only with my résumé proving that readiness, but I think the important thing here is that John McCain and I, we share a vision for America that includes energy independence.

Why do I think that the problem here is about a misunderstanding of how to determine causation? Miss South Carolina has determined the following things to be true:

> If students can't do something, they should be taught to do it.
> If students can't do something, it is because they weren't taught to do it.
> If students can't do something that it seems anyone should be able to do, then it should be taught in school.
> Reading maps is more important than whatever would have to be eliminated from school so that reading maps could take its place.
> These decisions should be made on the basis of statistical evidence of student's abilities.

But is any of this reasonable? Not only could one argue with each of these propositions, but it is fair to say that Miss South Carolina herself doesn't know that she holds these positions, that she hasn't thought about them, and that she might disagree with what she said if someone pointed this out to her.

In other words, she cannot reason well precisely because her beliefs indicate that she does not think about causation, and one can guess that she doesn't think about causation because no one ever tried to get her to do so. So she may very well be smart but she sounds stupid because she seems to be unaware of her own causal reasoning and is not very good at it. Being good at understanding causation and figuring what could possibly cause what and why is a hallmark of intelligence.

Intelligence can be enhanced by practicing the cognitive processes that are the basis of intelligent behavior and intelligent reasoning. One of these hallmark processes is certainly causation.

We could make Miss South Carolina smarter by teaching her how to determine what causes what and asking her to figure things out and explain them to others using a causation model that she could defend. Of course, it would have been better if this process started when she was a small child.

Now, with that in mind, let's look at the Palin remark. Palin was asked about her readiness for the office of vice president, which isn't much of an office really. What was really being asked was her readiness for the presidency, which was not unreasonable to worry about considering John McCain's age. She responded in a way that made clear that she has no understanding of causation either.

In the statements above, she asserted (implicitly) the following beliefs about causation:

Any mayor or city manager is ready to be president.
Any governor is ready to be president.
Any commissioner is ready to be president.
Any regulator of gas and oil is ready to be president.
If you have a vision of energy independence, you are ready to be president.

Now, of course, one of these beliefs is, in fact, shared by the country since we have chosen governors to be president. But the other beliefs are simply wrong. No one thinks that having a vision of energy independence prepares you to be president or that being an oil and gas regulator prepares you to be president.

So, what does Palin misunderstand here? She doesn't get the idea of preparedness as causation. Having a degree in accounting prepares you to be an accountant, most would agree. We believe, as a society, in certain rites of passage preparing you for the next step. Palin apparently has never thought about this or why anyone would hold such beliefs.

It is not an unreasonable question to ask whether being a U.S. senator prepares you to be president. It would not have been odd if Palin had asked Couric whether we ever had a president who actually was prepared for the job. Other than vice presidents who work closely with a president for 4 years or more, it is not unreasonable to assert that we have a history of unprepared presidents. But she didn't say that because preparedness is a causative notion and Palin doesn't seem to get causation. She may be bright enough to have been taught about causation when she was small, but apparently this didn't happen. As a result, she seems stupid to those who do understand causation.

Palin recently has made statements that make you wonder where her ideas about causation come from. This is from a 2009 interview on ABC:

Walters: Now let's talk about some issues—the Middle East. The Obama Administration does not want Israel to build any more settlements on what they consider Palestinian territory. What is your view on this?

Palin: I disagree with the Obama Administration on that. I believe that, um, the Jewish settlements should be allowed to be expanded upon because the population of Israel is going to grow. More and more Jewish people will be flocking to Israel in the days and weeks and months ahead.

What is the problem here? Again, there is a question of causation, but it is more obvious that that is the issue. No one who hears this statement would fail to ask why Jews would be flocking to Israel in the weeks and months ahead.

It is important to understand that determination of causation is the backbone of an intelligently thought out belief system. People believe certain things. They believe that the sun will rise in the morning and that their parents will come home from work at night. Beliefs often are based on observation and generalization. People also are taught beliefs. There are many ways to acquire beliefs. Children get them from their parents mostly but also from friends and siblings. At some point, however, reality comes into play. Reality often means comparing a belief with what you know or can figure out about causation. You can believe that the sun rises each morning but not know its cause. And, of course, you can learn the cause. You can believe that the

Great Pumpkin rises on Halloween if you like, but at some point you might notice that this doesn't seem to take place.

Beliefs, reality, and the rules of causation are interrelated but they are not the same thing. Causal knowledge should, however, enable one to alter erroneous beliefs that don't stand up to what one knows about causation.

So what would cause Jews to suddenly flock to Israel? Is she privy to information about another Holocaust or is this some fundamentalist religious belief? She doesn't say. The fact that she doesn't say, is what makes her look either unintelligent or incapable of clear reasoning. Being able to justify one's beliefs by citing common knowledge or revealing knowledge known only to you involves relying on commonly known rules about causation.

What about prediction?

You can believe that New York will beat Philadelphia in football. You can predict it based on evidence. You can explain the cause and effect that have made you come to this point of view. But, after New York loses, you need to modify some beliefs that you previously held. At the very least you have to acknowledge that your prediction was wrong and you might want take this into account the next time you make a prediction, by finding out what went wrong in your reasoning, if anything. Or, you simply can say your team wasn't lucky, of course.

Prediction relies on beliefs, and in many situations predictions are or are not verified immediately and new thinking can begin. But when one gets married, for example, one is predicting that the marriage will be good and will work out well for all parties. One might not realize for some years that this prediction was wrong. Then, when seeking a new marriage, the predictor hopes she has determined what went wrong by seeing what erroneous beliefs were held the last time.

It is very good to be able to predict, but predictive ability is not seen as a sign of intelligence. After all, people seek out fortune tellers because they think fortune tellers have a gift, not because they think fortune tellers are very bright. At the 2010 Olympics an octopus was apparently capable of making accurate predictions. No one claimed that it was an especially bright octopus.

A prediction made by someone that is justified by, "I just feel it," makes the predictor look foolish. In contrast, a prediction about relativity, for example, that is complex to understand but has been explained clearly and later is borne out by evidence makes the predictor look like a genius. But what actually makes us feel that a scientist's accurate predictions make him smart is the reasoning behind those predictions, the causal explanation.

We can see how intelligence, or the lack of it, is perceived by people and we must begin to reconsider how intelligence should be measured by those trying to put numbers to mental abilities. And, we can see why those Palin supporters seem so dumb. Let's look at one of them again:

> Interviewer: What do you think she would bring in terms of policy to office?
> Young woman: Good judgment.
> Interviewer: Any specifics?
> Young woman: I think she would control the out-of-control spending.

This is a prediction. The question is what this prediction is based on. It is a good guess that the young woman cannot cite examples of Palin's good judgment and has no idea whether Palin was able to control spending in Alaska. If she were able to cite examples, that is, if her predictions were supported by evidence that she clearly articulated, we would, in fact, think that the young woman was smart. Perhaps she is smart and perhaps the editor of the TV show deliberately cut out those responses. It seems unlikely, given the weird "czar" remark that followed this, but the point is that we seek such evidence when we make a judgment about someone's intelligence.

What about planning? Those who make bad plans are usually laughed at. Criminals who get caught by doing something dumb are always made fun of by the press. Bad planning makes a person look stupid.

Bad judgment, on the other hand, is more easily forgiven. When you make a mistake, you can always claim to have used bad judgment. Make the same mistake again and you begin to look stupid.

So, if we are interested in making people more intelligent, as opposed to more knowledgeable, it is clear that we need to redefine what we mean by intelligence.

Intelligence is the ability to diagnose well, to plan well, and to be able to understand what causes what. To do this one must be able to reassess one's belief system when new evidence is presented and one must be able to explain one's reasoning clearly to those who ask. And, one must have a knowledge base of relevant information to draw upon. But our education system, in concentrating only on the knowledge base and not on independent reasoning from that knowledge base, has ensured that the knowledge base remains incomprehensible to most people and therefore is immediately forgotten after school is over.

It would be a good idea to eliminate IQ tests as a measure of intelligence and begin to teach people to do diagnosis, to plan well, to be able to determine causality, and to clearly explain their reasoning to others.

Those that cannot learn to do this would rightly be called stupid, and those who can would rightly be called intelligent.

Degrees of intelligence would be about one's ability to do this for more and more complex issues in complex domains.

CHAPTER 11

Restructuring the University

It is a miracle that curiosity survives formal education.
—Albert Einstein

When I moved from Stanford to Yale, it was entirely because of the efforts of Bob Abelson, a psychology professor who became my good friend and wonderful colleague during the 15 years I was at Yale. Bob had been instrumental in helping to create the Computer Science Department at Yale, which is the department that wound up recruiting me (Bob had hoped I would be outside the department structure since I didn't really fit in anywhere very well, but he couldn't win that argument.)

Bob told me a story about the creation of the Computer Science Department at Yale, which involved his having to argue with another faculty member on a university committee about why a department should be created around a machine. He said that one member of the committee actually asked him whether there should be a department of lathe science as well.

We both found this to be pretty funny at the time. Now, however, I have to admit that the guy had a point.

I have been a professor in quite a few academic departments in my university career: linguistics, computer science, psychology, education, and electrical engineering. These departments all have some something in common: They have no real reason to exist. One would assume that departments represent academic disciplines that are coherent in some way, but it simply isn't so. The people in a computer science department, for example, have in common that they all think about computer-related issues, but so do people in other disciplines. Some parts of computer science have more in common with mathematics than they do with other parts of computer science. There were many people in the departments that I was in who worked on things that I didn't understand or care about. All our interchanges were about department affairs, never about computer science. We had nothing to say to one another about that. The same is true in every department. Academic departments are made up of faculty who have been thrown together for historical reasons but really have no business being in the same department.

What does a clinical psychologist have in common with someone who studies animal behavior? Do they talk about crazy chimps? What does an historical linguist have to say to a Chomskian linguist? What does someone who works on the philosophy of mind have to say to someone who studies religious philosophy?

Departments probably should have been organized around ideas instead of around words. I tried to facilitate that when I helped create cognitive science as a discipline by founding the *Journal of Cognitive Science* and the Cognitive Science Society. That was over 30 years ago and while some cognitive science departments have been created, in the end the disciplines that study the mind continue to do so in their own ways. Computer scientists who study the mind build computer models, and psychologists who study the mind run experiments. Anthropologists who study the mind do descriptions. That these are three of the twelve cognitive processes is no accident. Departments are organized to some extent around the processes that they use, but that is by no means the central organizing principle. As that old adversary to the creation of the Yale Computer Science Department said, the central organizing principle was a machine and that is kind of silly.

Who suffers from this state of affairs? The students, of course. When a department's faculty meets to decide what courses students must take in order to major in their field, it is not a sage conversation among scholars about what it means to be a computer scientist or psychologist. It is a political tug fest, where people from very diverse fields within these departments push and shove for turf.

Why do they care? There are two big reasons. First, if no one signs up for the courses you teach, you won't be teaching them for long. Second, if many students sign up for the courses you teach, you can justify hiring more faculty in your subdiscipline, which means more friends to hang out with and more power in department meetings where the votes can now go your way. You think this stuff doesn't matter? These issues are the lifeblood of every university department.

Let's look at both of these and see why they might matter.

Instead of subjects then, let's take a fanciful tour through the twelve cognitive processes and see what would happen to the university if it organized itself around those processes.

First let's look at the existing Yale departments and schools:

African American Studies
Anthropology
Applied Mathematics
Applied Physics
Architecture, School of
Art, School of
Astronomy
Biology
Biomedical Engineering
Chemical Engineering
Chemistry
Classics
Computer Science
Drama, School of
East Asian Languages & Literatures
Economics
Electrical Engineering
English Language & Literature
Environmental Engineering
Epidemiology & Public Health
Forestry & Environmental Studies, School of
French
Geology & Geophysics
Germanic Languages & Literatures
History
History of Art
International Relations
Italian
Law School
Linguistics
Mathematics
Mechanical Engineering
Medicine, School of

Music, School of
Near Eastern Languages & Civilizations
Nursing, School of
Philosophy
Physics
Political Science
Psychology
Slavic Languages & Literatures
Sociology
Spanish
Statistics

This list may be somewhat inaccurate since it is taken from a list of possible majors, which is not the same thing as a list of departments. I just edited it to reflect my memory of Yale, which could conceivably have added a new department or two since I was there 20 years ago (but departments are not easily created or deleted at Yale).

Now let's ask what would happen if we reorganized.

Which departments specialize in prediction, for example? Clearly, economics is about prediction, as is physics, and sociology, and psychology, and any branch of engineering.

Which departments specialize in judgment? Law does certainly. Medicine, parts of psychology, parts of anthropology, aspects of statistics, architecture, and art history do so, as do many others.

Which departments specialize in modeling? Computer science certainly does, as do parts of psychology. Engineering disciplines do and nearly all of the sciences do. Economics and sociology do as well.

Which departments specialize in experimentation? All of the sciences, plus psychology, do experiments. Economics and sociology people sometimes do them. Political scientists do experiments.

Which departments specialize in describing? The humanities specialize in this, as do English and Italian, and Near Eastern languages, and linguistics, and anthropology. Parts of psychology and medicine and law do as well.

Where is diagnosis practiced? In medicine, of course, but also in law, business, and engineering.

Where is planning studied and practiced? In engineering and in architecture certainly, but also in business, medicine, computer science, and psychology.

Where is causation worried about? Nearly everywhere. Anyone in the social sciences or in any practical discipline worries about causation.

So, should departments be organized around the twelve cognitive processes? Probably not.

It would be difficult to do and everyone would be against it. It is difficult to change what has always been in place. But those who study diagnosis would benefit from being around others who were doing diagnosis all the time. And those who are worried about descriptions would do well to hang around others doing the same. But it doesn't matter that much, really. In a research university, professors really just talk with people who are doing more or less exactly what they themselves are doing. Departmental seminars are social gatherings more than intellectual meeting places, since a talk on one subspecialty rarely interests those who work in different subspecialties in the same department.

But none of this really matters. Our research universities (of which there are maybe 50 in the United States) are doing very well, and my problem is not with them. It is with the institutions that claim to be educating our youth for the future and that employ professors who have a Ph.D. from a research university and who really wish they were still there. The research universities serve as professor training grounds that train many more professors who can do research than we possibly could need. These people then become professors at institutions where hardly any student intends to get a Ph.D., but they continue to teach the same Ph.D. training curriculum that they studied.

This has got to stop. The problem is not so much the universities as the high schools, of course. As long as college is seen as a professor training ground, then high school is seen as way to get into the professor training ground, and a nonsensical system evolves that trains high school kids to study what professors need to know. This has to end.

When students sign up for psychology at their university, they want to know what is wrong with them and their parents, and instead they study how to do experiments because that is what their professors learned to do in graduate school. When students take computer science in college, they want to learn to use the computer, but instead they study the mathematics of computation because that is what their professor does. When kids study chemistry in college, they are doing it in order to become doctors for the most part, but instead of learning chemistry that doctors need to know, they study the chemistry research that their professors are doing. When they want to learn business, they learn economics. When they want to learn how to write, they learn about literature. All of this happens because of the nature of the research universities' domination of our education system.

In order to fix our high schools, we need to get rid of departments based on rather arbitrarily defined academic subjects. We should organize universities around the kinds of work people do, where work means the kinds of thinking that they engage in, not the machines that they play with. Anyway that's my suggestion.

AN IMAGINED FIRST YEAR IN COLLEGE

We all know that what I propose will never happen. University faculty would stop such a proposal at every turn. So, in the name of reality, I want to make a suggestion that university faculty possibly could adopt.

Simply divide the 4 years that make up college into two parts. Dedicate the first 2 years to the teaching of the 12 processes and the last 2 to the study of the subjects that the faculty so dearly love. *Introduction to X*, which now dominates the first 2 years of college for most students, would be abandoned. The faculty hate teaching it anyway and the students hate taking it.

How would this work? Let's first consider the set of processes grouped under conceptual processes.

Conceptual Processes

Prediction is an area of life that is worth getting good at doing. Who, in the various faculties, organize their daily lives around predictions? Economists make predictions. It is what they do all the time. Medical doctors make predictions. Physicists make predictions. Political scientists make predictions. Let's imagine that students were taught by a team of people from these four areas who were exactly those people who specialized in making predictions all the time in their careers. And, let's suppose that they created a year-long course in how to make predictions based on known evidence, past cases, and pushing the boundaries of what is known. Wouldn't this be a better course than Introduction to Physics? The teachers could introduce whatever aspects of physics they wanted to help students understand the predictive process in that area, but other faculty who did prediction in other areas would be part of the discussion. There would be a set of interesting issues ranging from predictions that were thought to be right but weren't, to predictions that are being made today in each area. The content would be the predictive process itself, not the traditional subject matter. Statistics (and other useful tools) would be taught in this context while the predictive process was being studied.

Modeling. Who build models? Psychologists think about models of the mind, as do computer scientists and philosophers who specialize in thinking about thinking. Architects and economists build models of a different sort. Engineers work with models regularly. All of these people use different modeling tools but they work on the same thing: trying to figure out how something works by building it and seeing if they can replicate it. They may be using a computer or building blocks or electricity or art. It makes no difference. It is all an attempt to see how things work by building some facsimile. This is an important idea in human thinking, and a course should be taught to undergraduates on how to do it by the people who actually do it, teaching different techniques as they go. There are many ways to build a model, and students in college should know the possibilities before they take on further study.

Experimentation. Psychologists do experiments. Chemists do experiments. Physicists do experiments. Medical researchers do experiments. (The drug companies are constantly doing experiments that affect us all.) Why is there no course in learning how to do an experiment? Shouldn't students be learning how to come up with a hypothesis and how to test that hypothesis? Isn't that more important as a fundamental building block of the mind than any course offered to freshmen in college today?

Evaluation. Every academic field does evaluation. In every discipline there are ways and means to discuss and evaluate the worth of papers and research and practical proposals. Businesses are evaluated regularly and evaluation is taught explicitly in business school. Political scientists evaluate politicians and political systems. Historians evaluate what makes governments, battles, cities, and a range of other things successful. Architects and urban planners and engineers worry about evaluation of what they propose and produce. All of these people could combine to teach students how to evaluate. This is very important part of functioning in any society.

First College Year Summary

It would be my contention that a freshman year made up of these four processes, taught in four simultaneous courses that were designed to relate to one another in various ways and at specific times, would be a wonderful thing for teaching people how to think. The best of our faculty could teach what they thought about to students, who now would be ready to start to think rigorously. By the end of this first year, students could begin to specialize, not in academic subjects just yet, but in other processes that build on the conceptual processes.

SECOND YEAR IN COLLEGE

Let's look at the analytic processes.

Analytic Processes

Diagnosis. Who does diagnosis? Doctors certainly. Lawyers certainly. All the people I mentioned above who are building models need to figure out why their models may have gone wrong. Anyone who manages people or large operations needs to figure out all the time what has gone wrong. In fact, diagnosis is a critical part of nearly every area of thinking and every area of work. Diagnosis needs to be studied for its own sake. How do we do diagnosis in principle, no matter what the situation?

Diagnosis also needs to be examined in the various contexts in which it can be applied. A course in diagnosis, taught by the entire faculty who do diagnosis regularly, showing real work and real situations that they have had to handle, and coming after the first year, would have two advantages. One, it could build on the basic conceptual processes discussed above. Second, students could choose to think about diagnosis in some areas as opposed to others. Art experts might teach about art fraud, and lawyers might teach about detecting business fraud. In each case there would be similarities, and these should be taught by a group of faculty from different areas, but at the end of the course students should be able to start to actually do diagnosis under the tutelage of an expert in an area that interests them.

They actually may not know much about that area of knowledge, of course, and that would be the objection of the faculty to this idea. But it is my contention that faculty have had this wrong all these years. Teaching the basics to students, who have no concept of their possible use, is really not helpful. All these introductory courses are just an excuse to pack kids into lecture halls and pretend to do education while saving money on hiring more teachers. Teachers should pose real-world problems to students and encourage students to gain the knowledge they need to solve them.

Diagnosis is a perfect area for this. One can try one's hand at crime detection, without knowing everything about the details of how one does it, with the help of an expert looking over one's shoulder. This kind of just-in-time learning is how humans have always learned what they needed to know. The idea that school should teach you what you need to know before you need to know it, is seriously flawed. People can't remember what they learned, years after they learned it in school, if they haven't been practicing what they learned all along.

Judgment. Law typically is not part of any college curriculum because law schools are recent inventions on college campuses (that is, they are from the past century and not the century before) so law never got to be part of the required or even elective set of college courses despite the fact that so many students want to be lawyers. Judges make judgments all the time, and those lawyers who teach judges to make judgments should be teaching freshmen to make judgments as well. Of course, artists and musicians and literary critics make judgments of a different sort, as do philosophers and businesspeople. All of these people could be teaching a course together on how to make judgments fairly and how to determine what is fair. This is where ethics and morality come into play as well.

Planning. What I said about diagnosis is also true of planning. We plan in everything we do. There are economic plans, architectural plans, medical treatment plans, business plans, and so on. A computer program is a type of plan, and research plans are everywhere in a university. Writing these plans is not so different in principle, but in reality a business plan doesn't look much like a treatment plan. So there is the idea of a good plan and the understanding of what a plan looks like, what a plan's description ought to be like, in any area of life. You may think a business plan should look a certain way, but if the business community has a different idea, that idea will turn out to be right.

Students should have the opportunity to write all kinds of plans, learning about the principles of planning while learning about what officially is considered to be a good plan in an area of the real world that interests them.

So, as part of the second year, students should get to study planning, and then study successful planning documents, and then write plans and have them evaluated by the faculty.

Causation. Who studies causation? Everybody. Psychologists worry about what makes people crazy, doctors worry about what makes people sick, environmentalists worry about what is ruining the planet. Physicists want to know how the world works. Computer scientists want to know how computers can work better. Engineers do nothing but causation, really. So, here again, determining causes is a basic cognitive skill and it can be learned within the second year as well, in the same way I have been describing building on what came in the first year to tackle complex problems of causation in areas that interest the students.

Social Processes

Describing can easily be taught, as all of the eight processes discussed above are taught by requiring students to present their work in written and oral form. Students need to learn to write but they also need to learn to talk and to use alternative media to make their points and to explain what they have done. A coherent course of study in how to describe properly is easily within the ability of any college faculty and ought to be its highest priority, taught from many different points of view, teaching what description is about, not how to work PowerPoint.

THIRD YEAR IN COLLEGE AND BEYOND

Now what next?

After these 2 years, what will students be able to do and what should the faculty do with them? Clearly, faculty, as I have pointed out, want to teach what interests them—their own research subspecialties. Faculty will want to continue to insist on there being majors. Students should not have to be forced to select a major subject because majors (and, of course, subjects) are at the root of the problem.

Whose needs do majors satisfy? Faculty like them because the faculty can determine that to be a major in X students must know all of its aspects, and then insist that students, take obscure courses that they would not want to take. This is another way of making sure that faculty get to teach whatever they want to teach.

An alternative would be to let students specialize in a cognitive process, like diagnosis, and an area where they have become knowledgeable to which diagnosis applies, like financial diagnosis or behavioral diagnosis. Every student who majors in business doesn't really want to, or need to, know every aspect of business, and a student who majors in psychology doesn't need to study clinical, social, animal, and developmental psychology, if what he is interested in is diagnosing personality disorders, for example.

Let students specialize, if they want—they shouldn't be made to, but let them specialize in processes that they might want to become proficient at. We shouldn't force them to take courses that in no way serve their interests. Such requirements are made using arguments about breadth when they are there to make sure that undersubscribed courses get taught. Majors in computer science at Yale when I arrived there had to take artificial intelligence and numerical analysis. These subjects never interest the same people. They are as different as accounting and clinical psychology. These requirements were there because faculty wanted to make sure there were students enrolled in their course. If they didn't, they would have had to teach something they didn't know as well. Faculty made arguments about the well-rounded student, but students' needs had nothing to do with it.

Whenever you see a required course in a departmental major, there is politics behind it. Someone has traded with someone else. If you make them take my course, then I will vote to make them take your course. It is how requirements are created at every school. No one is thinking of the students' needs, trust me.

So what if we did think of the students' needs? What would we do in the third and fourth years of college? It seems obvious that students would like to learn some job skills and that they would like to be able to pick subjects that interested them for further study. In addition, they might have found something that they were working on in the first 2 years that made them want to get better at it. This is what the rest of college should look like then.

For computer science, for example, students should get to select software engineering, as suggested by my colleague earlier, if they want to be employable, and they should be able to improve cognitive skills that they may have acquired in the first 2 years. They may not have studied various subspecialties in computer science, so they should get to choose the ones that interest them. They also may have an interest in pursuing some noncomputer-related subjects taught at the university, for their own edification. In other words, they get to choose and the choices should include job skills and continued use of the cognitive processes they have honed in the first 2 years. Faculty simply should offer choices, and students should pick.

What would happen if this were done?

In a world where students got to decide what they studied, many of the departments listed above would disappear. There might be some call for Near Eastern languages or art history, but not that much. These departments exist for historical reasons and universities are reluctant to get rid of them, so universities make requirements that students take courses in them. An enormous English department is justified only by the sense that universities ought to have that sort of thing and by continuing English literature requirements for students. Without that, such departments would be much smaller than they are.

Therefore, it is clear that this cannot happen.

What could happen is this: High schools could change and colleges would have to adapt. This is possible because high school does not have to be the way it is today. Its current organization around academic subjects makes no sense. This can be fixed by simply building different kinds of high school curricula. But how can we change high school?

As it stands now, we can't. High schools teach what colleges tell them to teach. Recently I was looking for a picture of the man who was principal of my elementary school many years ago. I wanted to put it in a speech I was about to give. So, I went to the P.S. 247 (Brooklyn) website and discovered that it is now a "New York City College Partnership Elementary School." When I finished laughing, I started to wonder when this "everyone must spend their entire childhood worrying about getting into college" nonsense would end. P.S. 247 was not a great bastion of learning or a fun place in the 1950s, and I can only imagine how awful it is now. I wondered why P.S. 247 now had to be a college prep elementary school. A commenter on what I wrote noted that the old trade schools, which used to dominate the New York school system, were serving mostly minority populations and this had to stop; so now "everyone can go to college" is the mantra of the equity folks.

But the problem is, of course, that what is being bought with all this college preparation is the right to be an unemployed English major instead of the airplane mechanic you might have been if you had gone to Aviation High School.

High school has become all about college, and college is all about scholarship and research, so what is left? So who teaches students to think clearly? Who teaches students about the possibilities there are for work that might interest them? Who teaches students how to get along with one another, and who teaches people how to communicate well?

Certainly not the high schools, which are obsessed with test score preparation, which means rote memory for the most part.

Certainly not the colleges, which are run by faculty who do research and who think mostly about that.

One possible answer is community colleges, but when someone like me suggests that skipping college and going to community college instead to learn an actual skill might be a good idea for most students, that suggestion is disregarded as being on the lunatic fringe.

The good news is that because of all this craziness, there is a big opportunity to build an alternative, which I will discuss in Chapter 14.

CHAPTER 12

How Not to Teach

Some people will never learn anything, for this reason, because they understand everything too soon.

—Alexander Pope

My daughter learned a lot from me and from her surroundings when she was small. All children learn all the time when they are little. But what are they learning? When Hana was about 1-1/2 we lived in Switzerland. Hana was my parent's first grandchild. Since they were in New York, there were frequent phone calls back and forth and more than the occasional visit. Once during this period I got curious as to whether Hana knew the names of her grandparents. I figured she might not know the word *name* so I asked her, "What does Gammy (her name for my mother) call Poppy (my father). She immediately responded, "Maaacc!!" imitating the intonation and exasperation of my mother trying to get my father's attention. I asked what my father called my mother, and she said "Marge!" in the tone of an authoritative military call.

Hana talked to her grandparents on the phone quite a bit. One day I noticed her walking in furious circles while she was talking, at one point almost bringing the phone down on her head. Now who had been teaching her that? Well . . . me. That's what I do when I talk on the phone. And it is still what my daughter does, 30 years later.

Speaking of 30 years later (well, 20 in this story), I observed this same seemingly imitative behavior in Hana when she was in college. I remarked to a friend of my daughter who went to school with her in Evanston that there was a no left turn sign in Evanston (where I also worked) that I always ignored because it was so stupid. She said that my daughter always ignored the same sign and also said it was stupid. The curious part of this story is that my daughter and I, having our own cars and lives, had never been in a car together in Evanston and neither had we ever discussed this sign.

Did I teach her to ignore stupid no left turn signs? Of course I did. But I never said such a thing to her or taught her how to decide when it was safe to ignore a sign. I was just in her world and she was watching.

I observed a similar phenomenon with my son. I like to watch football and my son sat with me and learned to watch too. Twenty years later, when an event occurred on the field, I noticed that we said exactly the same thing at the same time. "Oof," "oh come on," "ugh." Whatever event on the field caused me to exclaim something, caused my son to exclaim the same thing. Now, I could not tell you what was an "oof" and what was an "ugh," and neither could he. I do this kind of thing unconsciously and so does he. He learned what I had to teach, but he doesn't know what he learned and I don't know what I taught.

What does this have to do with teaching? Perhaps we just need to watch our teachers and then we can copy what they do. Well, not exactly.

I took a yoga lesson the other day. The instructor got into a pose and said I was to copy what he did. I said there wasn't a chance that I could copy what he did. He wasn't used to being talked to like this. (Most students are better at being students than I am, of course.) I explained that I could barely understand what he had done, despite seeing it, and I certainly didn't know the intent of what he had done, so I wouldn't know which aspects of his action were significant and which were unimportant. I told him this was no way to teach.

Now I know I will not be able to teach the yoga instructor how to teach better, and I doubt he will be reading this book. But whether you are teaching yoga or baseball or science or business, the rules are the same. Before I list them, let me start with the top mistakes teachers make. Some of these mistakes are forced on teachers by a badly designed education system, and some are ones that teachers make no matter what they are teaching or which system they are teaching in.

Some of these are less than obvious. So, let's consider them one by one:

Mistake #1: Assuming that there is some kind of learning other than learning by doing

Mistake #2: Believing that a teacher's job is assessment

Mistake #3: Thinking there is something that everyone must know in order to proceed

Mistake #4: Thinking that students are not worried about the
    purpose of what they are being taught
Mistake #5: Thinking that studying can replace repeated practice
    as a key learning technique
Mistake #6: Thinking that because students have chosen to take
    your course, they have an interest in learning what you plan
    to teach them
Mistake# 7: Correcting a student who is doing something wrong
    by telling him what to do instead
Mistake #8: Thinking that a student remembers what you just
    taught him

Now, let's consider these teaching mistakes one by one.

Mistake #1: Assuming that there is some kind of learning other than learning by doing

All of us, teachers or not, believe that we can teach by telling.
When I say that people learn by doing, people think: Yes, maybe most
of the time, but you also can learn by being told. The issue is what it
means to learn, of course. I define learning in terms of the cognitive
processes that are exercised during the attempt to learn.

This means that when I say the following: "You cannot learn by
being told," what I mean is that that you cannot learn to do any cognitive process by being told. I can tell you that George Washington
never told a lie, and you could learn that and you could make it something that you now believe. But this is not learning in the sense that
it doesn't make you more capable of doing something because you
have learned it. Subject-based education relies on learning by telling
because for most of the things that are being taught, there is no other
way to learn them. How else could you learn that George Washington
never told a lie? By observation? By historical research? We learn this
by being told. But we do not learn cognitive processes by simply being
told. We learn them by practicing them.

This confusion is why teaching in its current form, with a teacher
in front of a class, exists at all. Without this focus on subject-based
education, it could not exist. And, this is why parents never stand in
front of their kids teaching them things. Cognitive processes cannot
be altered by telling.

So, we have rule #1 for teaching:

Rule #1: A teacher should never tell a student anything that the teacher thinks is true. Now, on the surface this seems ridiculous. How can you resist telling students the truth? Isn't that your job as a teacher? No. It isn't.

Why not?

Because, in general, students wouldn't believe you anyway. Students don't take what teachers say as gospel. And, they tend not to remember what you say. I have taught many a class and asserted X only to be told minutes later that I had asserted *not X*. People don't listen very well. So what is the point of saying true things, besides feeling good about having said something wise? The point certainly isn't teaching.

How will students learn what is true, then? By discovery. By failure. By repeated experience. By talking with people about what they think and having to defend their claims. Not by listening to you.

Let's consider mistake #2.

Mistake #2: Believing that a teacher's job is assessment

What does this mean? In the real world, teaching and assessment are usually conjoined. Teachers teach and they also give grades and test. This is a problem. It is a problem because satisfying the teacher becomes a goal of the student that tends to supersede learning, and it is a problem because as the ultimate arbiter of truth, a teacher gets to say what is true and students have to believe it. To fix this a teacher needs to not be in this dual role.

This is easier said than done, of course. I used to tell students they would get an A no matter what they did as long as they handed in the work that I asked for. This had the effect of having many students sign up for an easy A and having the administration become annoyed with how many A's I gave out. Both of these outcomes were entirely predictable. But what I did changed student behavior in the class greatly.

They often wrote about how much they wanted to please the teacher and how once I took that out of the equation, how much it changed their view as to why they were doing anything at all. For some, it had a very bad effect. They just didn't take the class seriously. Others took it more seriously than ever because they were the judges of their own work. (I asked them to defend their viewpoints to the class during class time so their friends were also judges.)

Of course, the system teachers teach in does not allow them to separate assessment and teaching. But it doesn't allow them to teach only cognitive processes either. For a cognitive process-based education system to work, teachers must be allowed to teach, and others should be the ultimate judges of success. Teachers need to help students get where they are trying to go and let others decide whether they have gotten there.

So, we have rule #2 for teaching:

Rule #2: A teacher should never be the ultimate judge of the teacher's own students' success. Here again, this seems absurd. But in the end, this separation of responsibilities is very important. Parents judge how well their children are walking and talking, of course. But the children are not anxious about passing their parents' assessments. The success is its own reward. And in the end, others judge how well your children speak. A parent is really there to help, not judge.

Let's look at mistake #3.

Mistake #3: Thinking there is something that everyone must know in order to proceed

This is, of course, the killer mistake. Go to any faculty meeting, or interview any teacher, and he will tell you that something is the basis for all that follows that, and if you don't know it, you can't proceed in the subject he teaches. Theory first is the mantra of nearly every teacher. The question is why this is so. I have been in arguments about this so often that I wonder why these views are so widely held.

Teach theory first, then practice. Because of this mantra, computer science majors often don't learn to program in a way that actually would make them hirable, and budding medical students drown in a sea of chemistry equations. Businesspeople learn about finance long before they learn how to run a business, if they ever do learn that, and psychology students learn about B.F. Skinner when what they really wanted to know is why they are so screwed up.

Why do teachers like teaching theory so much? I think that the answer is that it is orderly stuff, with official answers that the teacher gets to know while the students try to learn them. This puts the teacher in a powerful situation and teachers are comfortable with that. Teaching practice is much harder. There often are no right answers and many screw-ups, and the learning process is much messier.

Theory is a subject. Practice in a field means exercising the 12 cognitive processes we have been referring to, and because of that, progress is much harder to ascertain. You can test theory. It is harder to test practice. One can gain a lot of knowledge about what doesn't work while practicing and still produce nothing worthwhile. The lessons learned are harder to assess. Teaching theory makes all teachers more comfortable. Of course, theory means there is no doing, so no one really learns much. After they pass the test, they can forget what they learned with no consequences.

There is a big difference between knowing that and knowing how. Schools have always emphasized knowing that. The primary reason for this is that the stuff you can say you know is testable. But knowing how is much more important. So we worry that students don't know that George Washington was the first president, without asking what the use of that knowledge is. There may be a use for that knowledge. It doesn't come to me immediately what that use would be, but let's assume there is some use for that knowledge for your average student. If so, that knowledge should be taught within the context in which it might be used. There is, for example, a use of that knowledge for constructing a history paper about the origins of the United States. Of course, that itself may not be a useful exercise. In the context of doing that exercise, assuming there was good justification for it, that knowledge would be naturally learned. Natural learning of factual knowledge, learning it when it comes up, is fine, as long as it isn't being learned so that it can be tested. It is much more useful to learn knowledge when that knowledge enables you to do something, however.

There are endless books about what every 3rd-grader must know that use the idea that factual knowledge is the basis of the ability to read as their justification. Unfortunately, the writers of these tracts have misunderstood the cognitive science behind those statements. It is difficult to read things when you don't understand what they are about. But it does not follow from that, that the solution is to ram that knowledge down kids' throats and then have them read. It is much more clever to have them read about what they know and to gradually increase their knowledge through stories that cause them to have to learn more in order to make the stories understandable to them. In that case, the learning is in context and thus more natural.

Rule #3: Teach practice first, theory and facts second (if you must teach theory and facts at all). It is the rare course that starts with, let's build this now. Courses that start like that usually hold the students' interest, however.

Now let's move on to the next mistake.

Mistake #4: Thinking that students are not worried about the purpose of what they are being taught

When students ask what use algebra will be to them, they are told they will need it later. They are told this about any number of subjects that they are forced to learn in high school. The problem is that subject-based education is never about the potential use of those subjects. Those were the subjects at Harvard in 1892; that is the only answer that is true about why students are being forced to learn them. No one gives that answer. In fact, very few seem to know that answer.

Students have the right to know why they are learning something. "You will need it later," is usually a lie, so we need to stop telling them that. And, we need to think about what real reasons there are to learn something. If we cannot find those reasons, we really shouldn't be teaching the subject. But, of course, I don't think we should be teaching subjects at all, so my view on this should come as no surprise.

Rule #4: Don't teach anything unless you can easily explain the use of learning it.

Let's look at the next mistake.

Mistake #5: Thinking that studying can replace repeated practice as a key learning technique

Practice makes sense. When studying and homework mean practice, then they are good things. But rarely is that their intent. Unless, of course, we are talking about practicing test taking, which makes sense only if good test scores are the goal. I realize that good test scores are, these days, the goal in our society, as one would expect in any subject-based education system.

So here is rule #5:

Rule #5: No homework unless that homework is to produce something.

Now let's have a look at mistake #6.

Mistake #6: Thinking that because students have chosen to take your course, they have an interest in learning what you plan to teach them

Professors who typically teach courses that students have chosen voluntarily to take generally are under the illusion that students have come to the course hoping to learn what they intend to teach. Nothing could be further from the truth. Unless you are teaching human sexuality or how to get a job, or abnormal psychology, you generally can expect that students have very little interest in the content you are about to share and a great interest in the grade you eventually are going to give them. The reason for this is simple enough. Professors are teaching a subject.

Subject, in the university world, is a euphemism for profession. The profession of English professors is something other than teaching English—it is being a professional in some subspecialty in literature or some allied field. Similarly, a professor of psychology has an area of research within psychology that is his real profession. When a professor teaches, he is teaching how things work in his profession and he is teaching the basics of being in that profession. The percentage of undergraduates in a class that actually want to enter the profession of the professors is very small. Most have no intention whatsoever of entering the profession of the professors. So, they recognize instantly that what they are learning is very unlikely to be of use to them in their later lives. Some take it seriously anyway and some don't. But for the most part students really aren't much interested in what a professor is teaching.

They don't listen and they don't do what you ask them to do. Why not? They may be lazy, but that isn't the real reason. It may be true that they are taking four other classes, but that also isn't the real reason. The real reason has to do with the inherent value of work, which is one of the real issues in the transformation from subject-based education to cognitive process-based education. Students can feel, rightly, that they have read enough Dickens or have solved enough equations to satisfy the teacher or at least to satisfy their own needs in these areas. The problem is, as I stated originally, that learning starts with a goal and that the students' goals may not be the same as the teacher's goals. Since the students have no Dickens-related goal, and actually have a teacher satisfaction goal, they simply have misestimated what will satisfy the teacher.

Now let's consider real goals. Students do not stop driving a car because they are tired even though they haven't arrived where they are going. They do not fail to ask out Mary Lou on a date because they got bored talking mid-sentence. They do not give up on hitting a baseball mid-swing or midway through the game. People put in the effort required when they are working on truly held goals. Subject-based goals are almost never truly held. But cognitive process goals are nearly always truly held if the student is working on real things. If school wants to deal with artificial things (flying an air flight simulator instead of a real plane, for example, in order to learn to fly), then those artificial things need to feel very real and be very motivating.

Rule #6: Try teaching students things they actually may need to know after they leave school.

Here is mistake #7.

Mistake# 7: Correcting a student who is doing something wrong by telling him what to do instead

This one seems really weird. Wouldn't you tell someone to do things differently or what went wrong when you see them making a mistake? Most of us would because this seems a reasonable thing to do. It just isn't a reasonable thing for a teacher to do. A teacher needs to help a student think about what went wrong as opposed to telling him what went wrong and how to fix it. What do you think happened? Why did it happen, do you suppose? What could you have done differently?

Why does this matter? It matters because self-generated explanations are remembered more easily than explanations that we are told. It actually is quite difficult to remember anything you have been told. It is much easier to remember what you yourself have thought up, in part because you probably spent some time doing it, considered alternatives, and finally decided on an explanation, and then perhaps you tested that explanation another time. A self-generated explanation is a hypothesis, and hypotheses that we have come up with ourselves serve as the basis for learning. We tend to remember what we ourselves have said and thought more than we remember the words of others.

Rule #7: Help students come up with their own explanations when they have made a mistake.

Here is the next one.

Mistake #8: Thinking that a student remembers what you just taught him

I can't tell you how many times I have said *X* in a lecture or discussion only to be asked why I believed *not X*. Why does this happen? People really don't listen. They are not being annoying. They really can't easily listen. There is so much going on in their own heads while you are talking that it is remarkable they hear anything of what anyone says to them. Teachers live in a world where students are worried about the perceptions of their friends, events at home, and a million other things that have nothing to do with what a teacher is saying. A teacher simply cannot assume that a student will remember what he was just told. In any case, a teacher shouldn't necessarily be telling students the truth.

How could telling a student the truth be a bad idea? When telling is about facts, it is certainly a fine idea. But remember, I do not think that it is the job of a teacher to tell students facts. A teacher's primary responsibility is to get students to understand the world better and to help enhance their capabilities. Neither of these things happens through a teacher telling a student anything. Comprehension is an internal affair, arrived at by thinking. Ability comes from practice. Neither comes from a teacher. What a teacher can do is to encourage students to take on more and thus enhance their capabilities, or think more and thus enhance their comprehension. This means that telling a student a fact that he needs just makes it all too simple. Figuring out what you need is the real issue. Confirming what a student has discovered is a fine idea, but even that isn't always a matter of telling the student the truth. A Socratic teacher might deny what he knows is true in order for a student to defend a point of view and learn to be convincing. A teacher might fail to praise a student, even when she has succeeded, because the student should know that she has succeeded in any case. I am not suggesting that teachers never tell the truth, only that it isn't necessary to do it all the time.

Since coming to one's own conclusions is mostly how we learn, the real job of a teacher is to force students to come to sensible conclusions by confronting what they already believe with stuff that is antithetical to those beliefs. A confused person has only two choices. Admit he is confused and doesn't care, or resolve the confusion. Resolving the confusion entails thinking. Teachers can encourage thinking by making sure students have something confusing to think about.

Rule #8: Never assume that a student is listening to what you are saying or that what you are saying really matters.

What I have been arguing so far amounts to defining what I call *Socratic apprenticeship*. Learning by doing is facilitated by a good teacher, but that teacher has to be around when needed and has to know what to say and what not to say that will help the student think harder. The teacher doesn't provide answers—he just helps students find out where to look for answers and how to know whether they found the answers. Our current education system does not encourage teaching and learning to work this way, and I assume neither did the system that Plato was criticizing when he started to talk about learning by doing and Socratic teaching in the first place.

But something important has changed. We can now create apprenticeships online. It is possible to learn by doing in a simulated world set up on the computer that provides for human help as needed. We have been building what we call story-centered curricula for about 10 years now. Students learn within the context of an intense yearlong experience where they do only projects and produce deliverables that are commented on and improved upon by interaction with a Socratic teacher. We have produced them for masters programs at various universities, for high school programs intended to replace what is there now, and for corporations when they wish to create really effective training.

These curricula change how we learn and how we teach. Both of these need to be reconsidered in the wake of the disaster of an education system that we have created.

In summary, a good teacher does the following:

- never tells a student anything that the teacher thinks is true
- never allows himself to be the ultimate judge of his own students' success
- teaches practice first, theory second (if he must teach theory at all)
- does not come up with lists of knowledge that every student must know
- doesn't teach anything unless he can easily explain the use of learning it
- assigns no homework unless that homework is to produce something
- groups students according to their interests and abilities, not their ages
- ensures that any reward to a student is intrinsic
- teaches students things they actually may need to know after they leave school
- helps students come up with their own explanations when they have made a mistake
- never assumes that a student is listening to what he is saying
- never assumes that students will do what he asked them to do if what he asked does not relate to a goal they truly hold
- never allows "pleasing the teacher" to be the goal of the student
- understands that students won't do what he tells them if they don't understand what is being asked of them
- earns the respect of students by demonstrating abilities
- motivates students to do better and does not help them to do better
- understands that his job is to get students to do something
- understands that experience, not teachers, changes belief systems
- confuses students
- does not expect credit for good teaching

CHAPTER 13

How the Best Universities Inadvertently Ruin Our Schools

We have met the enemy, and he is us.

—Walt Kelly

It should come as no surprise to readers of this book that I never really liked school. I endured it. I didn't have the option to quit—an unthinkable idea in my household. In the end I even wound up with a Yale degree (all right, an honorary one—but it is printed in Latin). Truth be told, I did get a real Ph.D., but that was more a testament to my figuring out how to work the system while avoiding the draft, than it was a testament to my scholarship or academic prowess.

I became a professor, an unlikely job for someone who hated school, and I became an unlikely colleague who worked with people who, by and large, loved school. I spent 35 years of my life as a professor at the best universities in America, and still I hated school.

Somewhere in the middle of my academic career, about the time that my kids went to school, I began to think about how learning worked. (I was trying to develop computers that learned.) Since my kids also hated school, I began to wonder about why school was the way it was and why it really had so little to do with learning as I understood it.

Eventually I realized that I was part of the problem. I readily had found employment in a world that let me think about interesting problems all day and work with really smart graduate students. To pay for this life of the mind, I was required to teach every now and then. I never really liked teaching for exactly the same reason I didn't like being on the other side of the classroom. I didn't get the point. I talked. Students listened or at least faked listening, and then there were grades to be given out based on how well they actually had been listening. I didn't like this game any more as a teacher than I had liked it as a student. Who said that listening to what I happened to be talking about was an important thing to do? And, who said students should be graded on how well they had listened to whatever truth I was espousing? What if I was saying nonsense? I didn't think I possessed a direct line to the truth any more than I had thought that my own teachers did. The system didn't make sense to me as a student and it didn't as a professor.

But it was a very easy job. And the pay, despite what people think about professors' salaries, was pretty good.

How hard was this teaching obligation? At Northwestern I was required to teach one 3-hour-a-week course for 1 quarter every other year. This came to about 36 hours of work in 2 years.

Yes, really.

So, how was I part of the problem? Actually my light teaching obligation is the tip of the iceberg of an enormous problem. It brings up the question of how and why that light load works for a university, the answer to which sheds light on what is wrong with our school system.

How do the economics of a university work such that a professor can teach so little? That is an important question. But an equally important question is how it is that a professor, who is after all, in the mind of the public at least, a teacher, teaches so little and is happy about it?

People used to ask me, when I said that I was a professor, what I taught. I would always laugh. I would suggest that they ask me instead what I was a professor of, which was, of course, the only relevant question. I didn't teach much and when I did teach, I hardly taught computer science, which was actually what I was a professor of. I usually taught my view of how the mind worked. Sometimes I taught how education needed to be fixed. But, anyhow, as I have said, there wasn't all that much teaching going on in my life. Sometimes I taught more often than required of me, simply because I was feeling guilty. The rules said I didn't have to teach much but there were students, usually graduate students, who were thinking that as they had attended this university in part to interact with me, at least I should teach a course that included them at least once. So I did it because I felt guilty, not because anyone higher up in the university cared what I did.

I remember a Yale undergraduate who wanted an appointment with me. He was screaming in the halls, after he had been told that he could see a graduate assistant instead of me, that he had paid $20,000 a year (or whatever the tuition was at that time) to attend Yale and he damn well was going to see me. I did in fact see him because he had a point.

Professors are hard to find. There are many reasons for this. The first is that if no one makes them see undergraduates, so why should they? The second is that from long experience most professors have come to understand that when an undergraduate wants to see them, there typically is one of two motives. Either the student wants to argue about a grade he or she received, or wants to engage the professor in a conversation whose point is that the undergraduate is really a great guy or gal and will be counting on a recommendation down the road. Neither of these conversations is any too fascinating to professors so they usually make themselves hard to find.

The funny part of this story is that the student who was making the fuss had neither of those issues. He was exactly the sort of student professors very much want to see. He wanted to become a professor in my field. This is exactly who a professor wants to meet with. The conversation with him didn't start out about that exactly, but it was easy to see that he had real issues he wanted to talk about, science issues, the kind professors wish were on the mind of every undergraduate but rarely are. This student did in fact become a professor, the ultimate success story for the professor who guided him there. And, no surprise, he treats undergraduates who want to see him the same way I treated him.

There is a naïve conception on the part of students in a top university that their needs matter to the professors of that university. But the top universities are not structured in such a way as to reward professors who care deeply about students. If a young assistant professor spends too much time with undergraduates, there usually will be some wiser head who will counsel him against this behavior. Assistant professors must be concerned with getting tenure. Having the students like you has next to nothing to do with tenure at the top universities.

No one higher up in the administration of the university cared much about how much I taught. "Why not?" you wonder. To answer this, one has to understand how universities really work, why they work that way, what game they are playing, and who wins and who loses. The answers to these questions, well known by anyone in a top university, are, somehow, completely unknown to the general public. Outsiders don't ask how Yale works. They ask how they can get their kids into Yale. And therein lies the problem.

As long as the customers keep coming, as long as people will do anything to get their kids into Yale, Yale will not have to change. Now bear in mind that going to Yale isn't such a bad experience. This is not my point. But Yale's attitude (and every other top university's attitude) toward what those universities are inherently about is seriously harming the education of every high school student and almost every college student in the country. Yale doesn't know that it is doing this.

The faculty of Yale didn't wake up one morning and think that destroying the American education system would be a good idea. They never think that subject-based education is a bad thing. They are professors of subjects, after all. It makes sense to them.

Most of the Yale faculty doesn't think for even a minute about the U.S. high school system, or the community college system, or the thousands of other colleges in the United States. Yale professors are thinking about their research, ideas, and projects. Yale administrators are thinking about making Yale work better and about money and prestige issues. They are not thinking that the subject-based education that is the basis of the university structure has filtered down to high school for no good reason. They think that there is a good reason: to prepare high school students for college, namely to make the professors' lives easier when the students arrive at college.

They do not know they are killing education with their subject orientation. But they are, just as surely as if they had a plan to do so and were working on it on a daily basis. And, the parents who just must send their kids to Yale are regularly giving them the power to continue doing just that.

People who do not live and work within the confines of a great university imagine that professors are basically teachers, like high school teachers but more intellectual. They do not understand the collective mindset at a place like Yale, a mindset that the Yale faculty, for the most part, is perfectly happy with. They do not understand why asking what I taught was a funny question. They do not readily get, if teaching isn't a professor's main concern, what exactly his concerns would be.

To explain all this requires looking at the life of a typical Yale faculty member and beginning to understand the world in which he lives. We must begin by understanding the aims of the university itself. Universities are employers, after all, and professors, like any other employee, worry about what their boss thinks of them. Curiously, however, professors don't really have bosses in the traditional sense. I remember the provost of a top university complaining to me that with professors everything is a la carte. The provost is the guy who runs the university. What he meant was that he could not ask any professor to do anything without the professor asking what he would get in return. The traditional sense of boss is gone, of course, when the boss can't fire you.

The real bosses in the university system are your colleagues.

Huh?

Your colleagues can't fire you. But this is what they can do. In order to hire a new senior faculty member at Yale, we actually had to write letters, at the beginning of the process, to all the important faculty members around the world in the subspecialty in which we wanted to hire, asking them to rank the top ten people in the world in that subspecialty. If the person we wanted was not on that top ten list, we would not be able to hire them without proving why we couldn't get one of the people in the top ten and why we so desperately needed someone who clearly wasn't that good.

Top universities are caught up in a game they can't get out of that has two very bad results. The game is the superstar-prestige game. Top universities want to be number one. They want this very badly. University administrators worry about this on a daily basis. All hirings revolve around this issue. All professors worry about their status in the academic world at large. It is the coin of the realm in academia.

Although it does not obviously follow from this, one effect of this game is less than stellar education for undergraduates. And, incidentally, this game also has a disastrous effect on the nation's high schools. This is not at all obvious to professors and to the universities for whom they work. To understand this, we need to first see what professors do and how they think about what they do.

I will start by telling a story about someone I barely know. He is a professor of aerospace engineering at the University of Washington, which is in the top tier of state universities. I met him because I was working on creating a high school aerospace curriculum that I hope one day will replace some of what is now in high school for those interested in engineering. I asked Boeing to host a meeting to design this curriculum and they agreed. They invited some of their engineers as well as this professor, I brought some of my people, and we began to design a series of projects that would take students with no knowledge of engineering and after a year allow them to work on designing a 787. Such a project-based, real-world curriculum is, in my mind, an important improvement on the way things are done now in school.

At the very beginning of the meeting, this professor said that he hoped the outcome of this high school curriculum redesign meeting would be a curriculum that taught math and science better because the average student at the University of Washington that he encountered had very weak math and science skills.

This was not my intent at all and I told him so. I was hoping to allow high school students to have a year-long experience of actually doing engineering so they could decide whether that interested them or at least make use of some of what they learned in their later lives. As far as I'm concerned, there is too much math and science in high school now and I told him so.

Since no one ever says things like that, he was quite shocked. I asked him, since he thought entering college students who wished to study aerospace were deficient in math and science, why he didn't think it was his obligation to teach it to them? He replied that this was the duty of the high schools. His position then was that even though less than 1% of college students would study aerospace engineering, nevertheless every student in the country should be made to learn the math and science they might need just in case they might study aerospace engineering.

Of course, this is hardly a unique position. In fact, this stance is exactly the one in place in high schools today. Just in case you some day might need it, we will teach it to you.

What is the reasoning behind this point of view?

What is really going on here relates strongly to the teaching requirement issue I mentioned earlier. I had a light teaching load. This man certainly teaches more often than I did. To see what his load was, I looked him up on the web. Here are the courses he was teaching in 2007–2008 as I wrote this:

- A A 430 Finite Element Structural Analysis
- A A 432 Composite Materials for Aerospace Structures
- A A 532 Mechanics of Composite Materials

I had guessed what kinds of courses he taught before looking him up. The man is about my age, which means he has seniority, and he is obviously respected by Boeing, so he is a senior and successful man in his field. This means a small teaching load since the best professors teach the least. Three semester-long courses in a year is a light load at a big state university.

You might wonder, as an outsider to the ins and outs of the university, why the best professors teach the least. You also might wonder why I knew the types of courses he would teach and what I mean by that. I will explain.

To start this explanation, it is important to understand why professors are "rewarded" with light teaching loads. (Note the word *load*. This is the normal way this is discussed in a university.) I was given an extraordinarily light load at Northwestern for two reasons. One reason was that universities, like baseball teams, recruit so-called "superstars" (yes, that is how they are referred to in the university) from competitors. So Northwestern had to beat Yale's offer in my case. At Yale I taught one semester-long course per year, so Northwestern simply made me a better offer.

The reason both of these universities would even consider such a light load is that I earned money for the university. As I used to tell my children when they asked "why" questions, in the end it is usually about money.

I was recruited by Northwestern (in 1988), but I was really being recruited by Andersen Consulting. They offered Northwestern (that is, they offered me if I came to Northwestern) $30 million (over a 10-year period). Yes, that's right, $30 million. I think you can see that Northwestern didn't really care what I taught or when I taught it. They wanted that money. And, they also wanted the prestige.

Before I go too much further, I need to explain the prestige thing because it is very important. In fact, the prestige issue for professors and universities is precisely the root of the problem in our education system. This will take some time to explain, so let me start simply for now.

When Harvard plays Yale in football, they are battling for prestige. But the battle may not be on the field exactly. The real battle is in how powerful and important the alumni who attend the game have become and how big their respective endowments have become and who has the best chemistry department or business school. It is a real battle. The battle is for reputation. And, although it may seem silly to take this battle seriously, it is taken very seriously. There is no World

Series that determines the winner. The real determination is made by newspapers, or parents who want their kids to apply there, or potential donors. But the battle is real enough.

This battle was dead serious before *U.S. News and World Report* started publishing annual rankings. Now, it is the basis of how the university functions. When the current president was recruited at Northwestern, he essentially was told that his job was to get Northwestern into the top ten (in the *U.S. News* rankings). Northwestern was ranked 12th or 13th at this time. In his first year he succeeded. Why? Because Northwestern's football team won the Big Ten title and went to the Rose Bowl. Of course, he had nothing to do with that. But the following year applications doubled (or something like that) and that is a statistic that *U.S. News* uses, so presto, we were number nine. It didn't last. Neither did it make sense.

Recruiting me was like winning the Rose Bowl. Well, all right, not really. But a member of the Board of Trustees actually did say to me when he met me: "It's our star quarterback." I brought in money and prestige. It is natural to wonder who actually got the money that Andersen offered and what was done with it and why it was given out, and, while we are at it, what exactly it was I did all day if I didn't teach.

First the university's share. Every dollar of that $30 million went into Northwestern's bank account. Then they let me spend it according to certain rules. The first rule is called "overhead." The university charges an overhead rate on all contracts. The actual percentage varies and one of the first things I had to negotiate with Northwestern was how much their take would be. I don't remember exactly now, but they got about 30% of what I brought in. So, about $9 million of this money went into Northwestern's pocket. Do you see now why they didn't care how much I taught? They just wanted me there and they wanted that money. By the way, they also got the interest on all the money.

They also got the prestige. I set up a new institute that became instantly well known and was something the university could brag about. The Institute for the Learning Sciences was something unique. Northwestern had one and no one else did. Moreover, I might (and did) raise even more money for my institute. More overhead money. Yippee!

What did I do with the money? Mostly what you can do with this money is hire people. If you have a research agenda, something you want to build or accomplish, you will need help. If you want to build a rocket ship that no one has ever built before, you will need to hire folks who can contribute. I was trying to build educational software but the principle was the same. I hired programmers, researchers, assistants to do lower level work, video staff, artists, and, of course, graduate students.

And, now you know what I did all day. I managed this enterprise. Eventually my institute had 200 people working in it. I did what any person in charge of 200 people does. I set the direction and checked on progress. Also, I wrote books and thought deep thoughts. This is what any professor does who brings in grant money. I was just doing it on a larger scale than most.

All of this is about winning the prestige game. Any university wants pre-eminent professors. Universities want the best faculty so their name is mentioned a lot, so they get applications from students, attention from the media, and more grant money. That is what universities do. Teaching? Well, how exactly does teaching fit in with all that?

It really doesn't. Most professors agree that the university is a lot nicer place when there aren't all those undergraduates around. From May to September New Haven was an idyllic place. Smart people, good weather, interesting conversation. Then in September, thousands of young people, making a racket and expecting to be taught. But, therein lies the problem. Are students really expecting to be taught?

It doesn't take very long for a professor to learn that those brilliant Yale students, the ones who killed themselves to get into the place, may not be there solely to enter into the life of the mind. While everyone is thinking great thoughts and doing great research over the summer, professors manage to get themselves believing that the job of a professor at a great university is to be an intellectual. What they forget easily enough is who is paying the bills. And, they forget the real agenda of those who are paying the bills. They are reminded soon enough.

Students want courses to be easy, not bother them too much with work outside the classroom, and help them get a good job. Of course, I am oversimplifying here. Many students attend Yale to learn what it is that you, the professor, really know and want to teach. In 15 years at Yale I met a number of them. I remember their names because there weren't that many. We can hope that all professors have met their share of that type of student.

Most college students are 18-year-olds who are on their own for the first time. They are more interested in exploring themselves and their new freedoms than they are in working hard at intellectual pursuits. Every university has underground lists, written by students, about courses that are easy or professors who readily give good grades. The real agenda of the majority of students is to take school just seriously enough to graduate. If you offered them a diploma after 1 year, most of them would take the deal.

This all brings me back to our aerospace friend. Why does he want high schools to teach more math? Because he doesn't want to teach it. Teaching undergraduates becomes pleasurable at precisely the point where you can teach the very courses this man teaches. He is teaching highly technical courses, and, it is safe to assume, the students who are taking those courses are there with serious intentions. They want to become engineers and they want to know what he knows. So he may well enjoy teaching them. But he certainly would not enjoy teaching them calculus. There is a big difference in the experience of teaching when you are teaching people who plan on working in your field some day and when you are teaching a required course that students wish they weren't being made to take.

But why does it matter what this man enjoys teaching?

In the ideal university, the one professors at top-tier universities would have if it were possible, professors, who consider themselves primarily to be researchers in very specialized subfields would teach only work that directly related to their actual research or was important for preparing future researchers in their field.

Professors at Yale get to be professors at Yale because they are either potentially or actually the best in the world at something. While this might not actually be true, it is certainly supposed to be true. When a professor is proposed to be promoted (or hired for the first time) as a full professor at Yale, the chair of his department must address a meeting of all the other chairs and high officials and explain why the professor in question is indeed the best in the world at what he does. To do this, the chairs often have to define what he does extremely narrowly to have it be at all credible. Isn't there someone at Stanford or Princeton who is just as good or, perish the thought, even better than the candidate you propose? There better not be or this candidate won't get voted in. So, somewhere in every professor's mind is the idea that he or she is the best at something or for assistant professors, soon will become the best at something.

Under this kind of pressure, and this kind of egotism, a professor's first and foremost concern is attaining and maintaining that exalted status. Teaching future professors in one's own field helps maintain that status, so graduate students pursuing Ph.D.s are quite often taken very seriously. Teaching graduate seminars is intellectually stimulating, may help with one's own research, and is therefore worthwhile to do. But undergraduates are a whole different story. Very small percentages of them actually will become researchers in one's field. Professors are in the fame game. They worry about the prestige of their department and themselves. They care about this because they won't attract high-quality Ph.D. students unless they maintain that prestige. Undergraduates do not figure into this equation. Except they do pay the bills.

So professors have to teach them. And, someone has to teach those damn introductory courses that typically have hundreds of students in them. Why do they have hundreds of students in them? Because no one wants to teach them so making the sections as large as possible means fewer professors will have to teach them. And, why does our aerospace guy want high school to teach the math his students need? Because he certainly doesn't want to do it. He wants to teach esoteric courses about composites, which is his field. Teaching basic math would be worse than teaching Introduction to Aerospace. A great deal of work and no enhancement to prestige at all. And, there is a bigger problem. He can't teach math because the structure of the university doesn't allow it.

Math is taught by the math department. If everyone had to learn math, there would have to be an awful lot of math professors. While that sounds OK, it really isn't possible. Remember, at top universities everyone has to be a superstar or close. Math isn't that hot of a field. There aren't large numbers of people wanting to become math professors, nor is there a great deal of funding for math research. Remember, without outside funding as a possibility, a top university isn't going to want to create a big department. You get big departments, and lots of professors, only in fields that pay for themselves through outside funding. So math has to stay small. Solution—make sure math is taught in high school.

This solution makes everyone in the university happy. And, it shouldn't be a big surprise that the original idea of requiring algebra of high school students came from the president of Harvard and the chairman of the Princeton Math Department (in 1892). It has always been in the university's interest to push teaching the basics that are needed in college into the hands of the high schools so that the university professor's life is easier and involves less teaching that he doesn't want to do.

So, of course, professors want high schools to do a better job. The question is why high schools should care about what universities want at all. High schools have their own problems, or should have, but they have been convinced to ignore their problems and focus on the problems that universities have.

Parents demand that high schools prepare their kids for college, which really means help them get into college. Gradually the high school curriculum has become one giant entrance test for college. The idea that someone might not want to go to college seems very odd to most people. So, if the colleges say more math, then more math it is. But colleges are not saying more math in good faith. They are just having high schools teach what they don't want to teach.

But there are about 3,000 colleges in the United States and only about 50 top-tier research universities. What Yale needs may not be what the other colleges need. Why, then, is the tail wagging the dog? Yale says jump and everybody asks how high. Yale sets the rules. Yale says 3 years of math, and 3 years of math it is, even though higher math will not, or at least should not, come up in most college classes.

Does Yale know it is doing this? Do the faculty understand that by requiring that the high schools teach mathematics, they are causing massive numbers of dropouts and making learning a very stressful experience for most high school students?

I think the answer is no, but even if they did know it, they would do nothing about it. They have a university to run and they simply cannot change the way they operate. I can explain this with a story, this time from Columbia University.

I once had the opportunity to create courses for Columbia University that would be put online through a business I started that was funded (and then abruptly terminated when the dot com boom busted) by venture capitalists. I interviewed various professors at Columbia in order to decide which courses to put online. I wasn't trying to simply copy the courses they had but was trying to build learn-by-doing versions of them that would be more engaging than the usual lecture course and would try to teach real-world skills rather than the usual stuff one gets in an introductory course.

We decided to build an economics course and talked at length with the chairman of the Economics Department. We decided to simulate the experience that this man had had working as an economic advisor in the White House. The students played that role in the simulation and learned how economics is used in the real world.

All of this is really beside the point, however. I learned, during these conversations, that at Columbia calculus is required in order to be an economics major. I wondered about this, since the courses we were building never had any complicated math in them, so it seemed that calculus wasn't something that came up regularly in real-world economics.

I asked and was told that my observation was right and that calculus was required in order to ensure that there wouldn't be too many economics majors. As an insider in the university world, I understood this remark, but it needs some explaining for outsiders.

Columbia doesn't have an undergraduate business major. And, in New York City there are a lot of students interested in business. Columbia and other Ivy League schools think that business isn't an academic subject, so students shouldn't learn it until they go to graduate school. Columbia does have a well-respected business school, but, as I pointed out, no one really wants to teach undergraduates so they certainly aren't lobbying to teach them. (This is also true of medical schools and law schools, and it is why you never see courses for undergraduates in those fields despite the evident interest of the undergraduates.)

So, potential businesspeople at Columbia need to major in something and economics seems to them to be a reasonable second choice. (I am not really sure that it is a good choice but these are 18-year-olds making these decisions.) Thus, the Economics Department is flooded with potential majors. This seems like it would be a good thing, doesn't it? Students want to study what you teach. Isn't that good?

Well, not really.

Let us assume we have an economics faculty of 20 people, each of whom teaches three courses a year. So we can offer 60 courses. Sounds like a good number. But this has to include graduate seminars, and the faculty will be lobbying to have more of these and more advanced courses where they can teach their own specialty, as I have said. But majors need courses too. They might need 20 or more. This doesn't leave a lot for introductory courses unless the department runs enormous lecture courses that have hundreds of students. Now departments know that such courses are pretty awful things and they try to keep them down to a dull roar. But if you have hundreds of students wanting to take your courses, and you were set up with just enough faculty to handle 60 courses with fewer than 20 students in each class, you have a problem. Multiple sections of courses require multiple faculty and maybe even, God forbid, heavier teaching loads.

Simply put, if there are too many majors, all the specialty courses will overflow and you might need twice the faculty to handle them. The university is not going to let you hire twice the faculty in order to handle them. Why not?

Tenure is why not. Once you hire tenured faculty, they stay forever. Tenure is another one of those ideas that sounds a lot better than it is. One of its downsides, and it has many, is that you can't easily hire new faculty when you need to. There may be a jump in economics majors this year, but who is to say that this will be true next year? Universities move slowly.

So, the current economics faculty would have to teach more courses. They simply do not want to do that. They want to go back to their offices and do research and write books and consult with the government or big business, should they call.

Voila!

Calculus.

That will keep the little buggers out. If that doesn't work, advanced calculus. Who cares if those courses have little relevance for economics? They can always say it might come up some day. (It might.) Or they can say it teaches rigorous thinking. The real reason is to keep the numbers down. This is also why biology and chemistry are required courses for pre-med students, why statistics is required for psychology majors, and so on. Most departments will not admit to this, but that's why those things are there.

You never see this kind of thing in departments that have too few students. Too few students is the kind of problem that gets your department shut down. So, linguistics departments, which were started when linguistics was in fashion in the 1960s, are always under threat of shut down. They won't be requiring calculus. But they would if their situation changed. Instead, what they are doing is trying to explain why linguistics is calculus.

Huh?

When I arrived at Northwestern, undergraduates were required to take a math course in order to graduate. There could have been any number of reasons for this requirement—none of them having to do with interests or needs of the undergraduates.

In fact, diverting from that story for a moment, my secretary, who never went to college, insisted that her daughters go, so one of them found herself in an art history course that she hated and complained to her mother who in turn complained to me. Why does she have to take art history? She is a business major (at Hofstra), for God's sake, said my secretary.

Obviously, I replied, there are art history professors who are worried that no one will take their course and they will be fired (tenure doesn't apply in that case as tenured faculty can be fired if their department is shut down), so they have lobbied successfully to require it. She thought that was stupid and so do I. Now back to Northwestern.

Clearly the mathematics professors at Northwestern were similarly concerned. Of course, they made their argument, the same way the Hofstra art history professors did, one would assume, about these courses being necessary for a liberal education, but the real argument was about saving the department and everyone knew it.

But at Northwestern, this math argument had been made a long time ago. What was new was that linguistics, at Northwestern, had been classified as a math course! The reasons are clear enough. No one was taking linguistics at Northwestern and the linguists were scared. How they won the argument that linguistics was math (and thus an alternative to the required math course) is anybody's guess. Just remember that none of this is being done with the interests of the students as the real agenda item.

If you believe, as universities do, that the most important thing you can do as an administrator is recruit superstars to make your university great, then there is a consequence to all this. The students suffer. At first this seems an odd idea. How could a student be harmed by recruiting a superstar? Well, it depends on the university.

At MIT, where students are different than they are at Northwestern by quite a bit, there are a number of superstars that I know quite well. Two of them, whom I will not name but are about as famous as a professor can be, are people I have heard lecture many times. I have never understood what they were talking about in any of those lectures. Now, bear in mind that I know their fields very well so I should have been able to understand them. Also, bear in mind that I was a terrible student, which means my attention fades fast when I am bored or irritated.

Since I know these two men well enough, I can tell you that neither is particularly worried about being understood. They have been acclaimed by one and all to be brilliant, and many brilliant people think that if you can't understand what they are thinking about, then it is your fault not theirs. They are talking about complex issues that interest them, and you should be able to follow along, and if you can't then you are a dope.

This works at MIT, sort of. No MIT student happily admits to not understanding what the professor is saying. They all muddle through as best they can and are usually awestruck by even being in the presence of these great men, much less being able to take a course from them. Understanding what they said, or, worse, actually being able to make use of what they said, seems unimportant by comparison. You would take a course given by Einstein, wouldn't you, even if you didn't understand physics? That is the attitude.

This attitude works at MIT. But it fails miserably at lesser schools.

I took advanced calculus from a superstar when I was an undergraduate. I didn't understand anything. I was a math major, but that course caused me to lose interest in math and start thinking about other things. I went to see this superstar and asked him for advice. We had a great conversation. He was a very smart guy. He pointed me in a direction that helped me make some important decisions. As a one-on-one advisor he was great. But the system made him teach, which really wasn't something he could do very well.

As luck would have it, years later when I was chairman of the Computer Science Department at Yale, he was one of my faculty. So, in a sense he wound up working for me (to the extent that any faculty member actually works for the chair, which is really not the case).

He was a great man. He inspired many a graduate student to become a professor. He was fun to talk to. But he couldn't teach at all. At Yale we made sure that he taught only specialty courses, which was fine with him. What he was doing teaching advanced calculus that year long ago is anybody's guess. My guess is that as he was the chairman of the Math Department at the time, either he got stuck with it because there was nobody else or he was trying to prove a point in order to induce senior faculty to come down from on high and teach the basics.

Either way it was a terrible idea.

Prestigious universities that recruit superstars are not, at the same time, recruiting teachers. They are just hoping someone can and will teach. But no one cares that much.

I once had dinner with a man who was on the Board of Trustees of the University of Illinois. I asked him how he liked being on the board of a fraudulent institution. He reacted the way you might expect and demanded an explanation. I asked him if he thought the average student attending the University of Illinois was going there because she figured after graduation she would be able to get a job.

He agreed.

I then asked whether job skills were in fact taught to the majority of students there and whether the faculty, by and large, actually had ever worked any place but a university.

He laughed.

It is OK that Yale hires only intellectuals and only the best of the best because Yale is not a state-run institution, and Yale can do what it wants. No one is making anyone go to Yale. Caveat emptor.

But a state spending a great deal of money on its flagship educational institution ought to know what it is getting.

This is what it is getting—Yale.

There are no faculty members at the University of Illinois in any mainstream department (I don't mean agriculture, for example) who do not consider themselves the equal of, and in some cases better than, their Yale colleagues.

When I went to Northwestern, I was given the right to hire a variety of faculty in a number of disciplines that related to learning. When you recruit faculty, you mostly consider how your institution might look better to someone at another institution. So, Northwestern doesn't recruit from Harvard or MIT (or Yale!) very often because Chicago doesn't seem a more appealing place than Boston to an academic and Northwestern isn't a step up. And, Northwestern doesn't recruit from California in general, for the same reason.

So, it's the University of Illinois!

I recruited heavily from Illinois because Chicago looks more appealing than Champaign-Urbana to most people, so I had something to offer, and the faculty there had already bought into the idea of living in the Midwest. Moreover, in the academic world, the University of Illinois is considered to be a top-ranked institution with a faculty every bit as good as Yale's, maybe better in some departments.

So, why is this bad?

It is bad for the students of the state of Illinois who worked hard to get into the state's best university only to discover that its faculty think they are at Yale.

Of course, they know they are not at Yale, but they are competing in that world nevertheless. They also do research and publish and work hard to be famous superstars. They are in exactly the same game as their Yale counterparts, so it follows that they don't want to teach either.

But the numbers are much bigger at Illinois. Classes are larger and faculty have to teach more classes. So these same people, who would readily move to an institution that didn't treat them like this, are stuck competing with their Yale colleagues and, at the same time, having so many more undergraduates to deal with.

Guess who loses?

And, I haven't even started to discuss the idea that most students at Illinois do not go there to become professors or intellectuals, or hobnob with the best and brightest. The faculty think they are (or ought to be) at Yale, but the students do not. The students want to get jobs 4 years later. Good luck with that. That is not what Yale is for.

I was told that explicitly one day, by the way. I had to give a short talk to entering freshmen at Yale when I was the department chair. The idea was to extol the virtues of majoring in the field represented by the chair. Each chair gave a short speech. Mine, as usual, was the shortest. Major in computer science—get a job. That was my speech.

I was booed.

I was booed by the freshmen, who by this time at Yale had been there maybe 5 minutes but had already absorbed the zeitgeist of the place. Yale was for thinkers not workers.

By the way, that was in 1982 or so. All our computer science graduates went to work at Microsoft in those years. There were lots of millionaire alums not too long after. (Presumably, not those who were booing.)

They wouldn't have booed at Illinois, and that is the point. Yale is not the problem unless you realize that it sets the direction for every other university in the country. It doesn't do this by itself and it doesn't do it intentionally. Nevertheless, it ruins the chances that Illinois graduates will receive a reasonably practical education that actually might get them jobs or teach them how to live in the real world.

So, we have created a system that values heavy intellectuals and gives them a place to do their thing. Is this bad? How could it be bad? It certainly isn't bad for the intellectuals. But it is bad for the students. Not necessarily for the students at Yale, although there are certainly unhappy students there. It is bad for the society at large. Students don't need to major in subjects unless they intend to become professionals in those subjects. Actually, they need to intend to be professional researchers in those subjects, since the faculty really don't know how to or care to think about their subject as anything other than a research area. Making a real living with what they teach is not on any faculty member's mind. But students go to college precisely because they think they will get a job afterward that college will have prepared them for. It just isn't true.

Teaching how to survive in the real world is simply not the job of an Ivy League professor. This is too bad because there are professors who really do like to teach.

One day I decided that I needed some news video from the major networks for a project I wanted to start. I called the president of Northwestern and asked him if he knew anyone at the networks, and he told me that the former president of one of them was now on our journalism faculty.

So I called him. He said he would help me but only on one condition. He wanted me to sit in on the class he taught. This was really an odd request, and especially hard for me to agree to given how much I hate classes and classrooms. But I really wanted that video.

Professors almost never ask other professors to watch them teach. One reason is that they usually aren't all that proud of their teaching and don't want to hear the criticism that inevitably follows. Also, it really isn't something they want to talk about even if they are good at it. It has minor value in a professor's world.

The class I attended was the most extraordinary I had ever witnessed. This former head of a network previously had been head of the news division. He had turned his class into an all-day simulation of a network newsroom. Students were charged with preparing and producing the evening news. They got their information from various sources that were used by the networks and prepared stories, played the roles of on-air reporter, news writer, anchor, camera person, editors, and so on. They finished and went on air at 5.00. At 5:30 they watched to see what the networks had done that day and compared and judged their own success. The professor was there all day guiding them.

I thought this class was fantastic and said so. I then said it would be a loss when he left Northwestern in a couple of years. He said he had no intention of leaving, but I knew what he was doing would never be tolerated.

Why not?

Let me count the reasons. First, he was teaching doing and practice, and not theory and analysis. While the rest of the world knows that doing and practice is how you learn, this is the exact opposite of how teaching occurs in a great university. (There are exceptions to this, of course. In engineering, agriculture, and even in journalism, practice does occur. But it always occurs in the presence of lots of theory.)

University professors are not practitioners. Usually they don't know a thing about how what they teach actually is used in the real world, never having been in the real world themselves, so they have created a culture where theories and ideas are considered to be more important than simply being able to do something. So one reason his class would have to go is that it inevitably would be seen as threatening to the other faculty.

Another reason that it threatens the other faculty is that it is a lot of work to do what he did. He was there all day. Professors teach 3 hours a week, 6 if they aren't superstars. No one wants to see a new standard of teaching created that is both practical and takes a long time to do. When would the professors do their research and write their books? This man didn't have that agenda. He just wanted to teach. There is no room for that in a top-tier university.

And, how would this class fit in a student's schedule? Students can't spend all day at something without missing those important required classes that meet 3 times a week for an hour. Totally consuming classes that take all day, and may even take all week, cannot possibly exist.

Two years later this man was gone.

It is actually very difficult to change the way a university runs, and this includes trying to change any aspect of how courses are offered or structured.

I learned this when I took on the job of building a new West Coast campus for Carnegie Mellon University. (By building, I mean designing its offerings, not its buildings.) As I am an advocate of learning by doing, in just the way our former network head was doing in his class, I decided that there would be no courses, only projects, and that each project would build on the one that preceded it. The administration in Pittsburgh let me get away with this precisely because there were no faculty hired in California and the Pittsburgh faculty wouldn't much notice what we were doing 2,000 miles away.

We had to lie to the registrar about what we were doing because courses had to be in parallel to make it into their system and we weren't offering courses at all. The projects had to be labeled as courses, but they varied in length (not every project takes the same amount of time). These "courses" ran in sequence not parallel, so we basically had to lie about it to get by the registrar.

The students objected that there were no faculty around and were no classes, so they felt cheated in some way and asked why they had to show up at all. We replied that they didn't, since all the materials they needed were online anyway. The students were assigned mentors who were on campus, but after a while students interacted with them by instant message instead of walking down the hall even when the students were on campus. The students started out hating what we did and wound up loving it. These were students in master's degree programs and they were, in essence, simulating the jobs they were preparing for.

Even the faculty in Pittsburgh came to appreciate what we were doing in California. But you will never hear about it (except from me). Carnegie Mellon will never brag about it or publicize it in any way.

Why not?

What I did is very threatening. At one point the provost, realizing that since the program was online, in principle we could serve a lot of students, asked me whether I was going to put Golden Arches over the campus and say over a million served. Seemed a good idea to me. But not to Carnegie Mellon. We don't want to cheapen our brand name, the provost told me.

In other words, if hundreds of thousands of people had Carnegie Mellon degrees, how prestigious would such a degree be? These degrees were in computer science, a field in which Carnegie Mellon is number one or two in the world. But if too many people had these degrees, the university's prestige would go down, so whether or not this was good educational practice, and the certifying boards certainly thought it was, this was never going to happen.

I made the mistake of saying in an interview how well our experiment was going, and was told by Carnegie Mellon to stop doing that. It seemed that parents of undergraduates at Carnegie Mellon were calling and asking why, if this method was so preferable to the usual course-based method, it wasn't being employed in Pittsburgh? Since that could never happen—the professors would never allow it—I had to stop giving interviews.

As I write this, the learn-by-doing master's degree programs we built are still running, but no more will be developed at Carnegie Mellon. Eventually the ones I built will be shut down. The reason will be that they employ teachers who teach (as mentors) all the time and therefore don't do research and that can't be allowed. Not if you are in the superstar prestige game.

Universities will not change until some equally prestigious online university is developed that challenges their ability to attract students. As long as students show up at Yale, and there is no danger there in the foreseeable future, Yale does not have to change.

But Yale must understand what it is doing to the high school system. It has to stop telling the high schools what to teach. It has to stop talking about how high schools must prepare students for college. That should not be its job. Yale has to accept the idea that students will arrive at Yale "unprepared" for college. Making Yale's admissions process easier should not be the job of the high schools. Teaching the subjects that superstars don't want to teach should not be the job of the high schools. High schools need to focus on the concerns and issues of real students living in the real world. If Yale really believes in algebra for its students, then it can teach algebra to all entering freshmen. (Believe me, it never will.)

Until subjects cease to be the basis of the structure of universities, there will be a big problem in education across the planet because everyone everywhere assumes that university degrees are important. As long as we assume this, and as long as we accept that what is taught in high school will be determined by the universities, we are in serious trouble. High schools have become college preparation centers and thus no one learns anything but academic subjects in high school.

Cognitive processes must be the meat of high schools and should be the basis of college as well. The top-tier colleges will not change and maybe they shouldn't. They can continue to be research universities and specialize in producing the next generation of Nobel physicists or literary scholars. Great scientists are nice and I am all for producing them. But the 3,000 colleges in the United States are not all producing great physicists. Still they teach chemistry and require mathematics for no reason that anyone can remember.

If we don't start thinking seriously about how to teach thinking, as opposed to academic subjects, to the 99% of students who have no intention of becoming scholars, we will all lose.

CHAPTER 14

What Can We Do About It?

Simple solutions seldom are. It takes a very unusual mind to undertake analysis of the obvious.

—Alfred North Whitehead

What is obvious here? Schooling is broken. It needs to be rethought. What can we build as an alternative? It is a simple question really. If we had all the resources in the world and we really wanted to educate our children, where education means teach them to think clearly, live well-thought-out lives, and be able to pursue their dreams, what would we build?

It is, of course, very difficult to think about replacing sacred institutions. The only way I know to think about it, is as a thought experiment. Just imagine that we lived in a different world, maybe a Greek colony in the 1st century, and ask yourself how we might educate our children in this environment, pretending that schools are the one thing we cannot build for some reason. As we think about this, we must not assume that what we teach in schools now needs to be taught in some other way. We simply need to ask: *What should one teach children?* while making no assumptions that what we have been teaching is necessarily relevant.

To put this another way, the right question to ask is: *What do children need to be able to do, in order to function in the world they inhabit?* The next question is, of course, How would we teach children to do those things?

Now admittedly I am prejudicing the answer here by simply leaving out the word *know*. The usual question is, What should children *know*? It is this question that leads people to make lists of things every 3rd-grader should know and allows school boards to create lists of facts students need to be tested on. So, let's leave that word out of the discussion and see where it gets us.

A good place to start is to ask what a highly functioning adult can do and moreover has to be able to do in order to live in this world. When we ask this question, the phrase "21st-century skills" will not come up. Every time that phrase comes up, somehow the answer turns out to include algebra and calculus and science, which, the last I heard, were 19th-century skills too.

In fact, let's not talk about particular centuries at all. To see why, I want to diverge for a moment into a discussion of the maritime industry, a subject with which I have become more fascinated over the years. What did a mariner from Ancient Greece have in common with his modern counterpart in terms of abilities?

The answer is an obsession with weather, ship maintenance, leadership and organization, navigation, planning, goal prioritization, and handling of emergencies.

Effective mariners from ancient times would have in common with those of today is an understanding of how to operate their ships, the basic laws of weather, tides, navigation, and other relevant issues in the physical world, and an ability to make decisions well when circumstances are difficult. They also would have to know how to get along with fellow workers, how to manage the people who report to them, as well as basic laws of commerce and defense.

In fact, the worlds they inhabit, from an educational point of view, that is, from thinking about what to teach and how to teach it, would be nearly identical except for one thing: how to operate and maintain the equipment. Their ships were, of course, quite different.

So, let's reformulate this question that seems to haunt every modern-day pundit on education (usually politicians or newspaper people). What are 21st-century skills? Can this question be transformed (for mariners) into what does a 21st-century mariner need to be educated about that his Ancient Greek counterpart was not educated about?

The answer, it seems obvious to me, is 21st-century equipment and procedures: engines, navigation devices, particular political situations, computers, and so on. But, and this is an important "but," none of this stuff is the real issue in the education of a mariner. The real issue is decision making. What one has to make a decision about is secondary to the issue of knowing how to make a decision at all.

You can learn about a piece of equipment or a procedure by apprenticeship. Start as a helper and move on gradually to being an expert. But this is not what school emphasizes. School typically attempts to intellectualize these subjects. Experts write books about the theory of how something works and the next we know, schools are teaching that theory as a prelude to actually doing the work. Scholarship has been equated with education. You do not have to know calculus to repair an engine. You might want to know calculus to design an engine, but that is no excuse for forcing every engineer to learn it. Similarly, you do not have to know theoretical physics to master the seas. Mariners do know physics, of course—practical physics about load balancing, for example—but they do not have to know how to derive the equations that describe it.

What I am saying here about the shipping industry holds true for every other area of life as well. Twenty-first-century skills are no different from 1st-century skills. Interestingly, Petronius, a 1st-century Roman author, complained that Roman schools were teaching "young men to grow up to be idiots, because they neither see nor hear one single thing connected with the usual circumstances of everyday life." In other words, schools have always been about educating the elite in things that don't matter much to anyone. This is fine as long as the elite don't have to work.

But today the elite have extrapolated from what they learned at Harvard and decided that every single schoolchild needs to know the same stuff. So, they whine and complain about math scores going down without once asking why this could possible matter. Math is not a 21st-century skill any more than it was a 1st-century skill. Algebra is nice for those who need it, and useless for those who don't. Skill in mathematics is certainly not going to make any industrial nation more competitive with any other, no matter how many times our "experts" assert that it will. One wonders how politicians can even say this junk, but they all do.

Why?

My own guess is that, apart from the fact that they all took these subjects in school (and were probably bad at them—you don't become a politician or a newspaper person because you were great at calculus), there is another issue: They don't know what else to suggest.

Thinking about the 1st-century will help us figure out what the real issues are. People then and people now had to learn how to function in the world they inhabit. This means being able to communicate, get along with others, function economically and physically, and in general reason about issues that confront them. It didn't mean then, and doesn't mean now, science and mathematics, at least not for 95% of the population.

How do we choose who studies the elite subjects? We don't.

Offer choices. Stop making lists of what one must know and start putting students into situations where they can learn from experience while attempting to accomplish goals that they set out for themselves, just as people did before there were schools. Education has always been the same: learning from experience with help from wiser mentors. School has screwed that all up and it is time to go back to basics.

So the "what" question is simple. We should teach children what adults know that enables them to function in the world they inhabit. This has much less to do with academic knowledge than it has to do with practical, and often subconscious, knowledge of how to do a variety of things in the social and physical and economic world we have created.

Now let's address the question of how to teach these things.

John Dewey noted, in 1916, that he had been talking about learning by doing for a long time, but nobody ever listened to him about it—which was exactly his point. He was frustrated about changing the system. In 1916! Imagine how he would feel today.

It is not unreasonable to ask why the system never changes, and who is making sure that it won't change. The answer is obvious. So many people have vested interests in things staying as they are that the system basically cannot change—at least not of its own free will.

The President of the United States could help make the changes needed, but he won't. Here is a piece from then-Senator Obama's education speech given during his campaign in Dayton, Ohio, in 2008:

> We will help schools integrate technology into their curriculum so we can make sure public school students are fluent in the digital language of the 21st-century economy. We'll teach our students not only math and science, but teamwork and critical thinking and communication skills, because that's how we'll make sure they're prepared for today's workplace.

Some advisor of his had read my writings and was quoting me on that one. I usually say reasoning and not critical thinking, but this is taken from my many speeches on education. And what has the President actually done? He said in that same speech:

And don't tell us that the only way to teach a child is to spend most of the year preparing him to fill in a few bubbles on a standardized test. I don't want teachers to be teaching to the test. I don't want them uninspired and I don't want our students uninspired.

Uh huh. Did he change No Child Left Behind? No. Of course not. Testing dominates education as much as it ever did. All presidents are the same, really. They can't fight the vested interests, or won't. I will avoid figuring out why here, although, once again, John Dewey had much to say on the subject of how governments stay in power by making sure that people aren't really educated.

We can't count on politicians, but here is what we can do. We can build it and then we can work inside or outside the system in such a way that allows people to be able to come.

But how do you build a new high school system? Very simple: one curriculum at a time. The trick is making sure that you put the curricula online. We cannot change education one school at a time. Many good schools have been created over the years. Today, John Dewey's Lab School (in Chicago), which was entirely a learning-by-doing place, is now a college prep school. Having a few reasonable schools will not change the system. A curriculum offered online is available to everyone and eventually can provide an alternative to a system that offers boring and mindless education.

In addition, *online* means *choices*. Once we create dozens, maybe hundreds, of curricula from which to choose, students should be able to learn anything they want to learn without regard to whether a teacher for that curriculum or other students interested in that curriculum happen to live nearby.

So, in an ideal world, what would these curricula be about?

They can be about anything that one can learn to do in the real world (which would leave out all the traditional academic subjects). They should teach teaching cognitive processes, of course, but one should not endeavor to teach cognitive processes specifically, that is, apart from their possible use. So, it is the use of these processes in some area of real life that would be the intent of any full-year, story-centered curriculum.

These curricula and any others that we would design have the following characteristics:

1. They must be learn-by-doing curricula consisting of series of projects inside coherent stories about life in some aspect of the real world.

2. They must be delivered on the web. Students should work on projects where the background and help are web delivered. They would submit their work to mentors and receive feedback online.

3. Mentors in the curricula would include parents, online subject matter experts worldwide, local experts, and teachers trained to be mentors. Mentoring, unlike teaching, is not about providing information that can be found easily in books but about helping students through a problem without giving them the answer. Mentors point students in the right direction and react to their work as it progresses.

4. Students should, on a regular basis (sometimes weekly, sometimes more often), submit work products related to each project for evaluation and feedback. Students would submit their work many times to achieve increasing mastery and get continuing feedback. There should be no competency tests, only the continual monitoring of performance.

5. Each curriculum should be designed by a panel of experts in a given field. The curriculum should provide a simulation of what life might be like in that field. For example, students might spend the year working legal cases, or starting a business, or designing roads and bridges.

6. Students should be encouraged to work in virtual teams, learning to deal with others to produce results.

7. Choice must be a staple of the curricula. There can be no single set of standard requirements. Instead, students should be able to select the curricula they wish to participate in. Their records would list what deliverables they have created in their chosen curricula.

8. Curricula must be designed around projects with clear, meaningful, achievable goals. They must be designed carefully so to incorporate all the key basic skills like reading, writing, reasoning, researching, calculating, computing, and so on, in a systematic and natural way.

Here are some curricula that have been proposed that would meet student's interests head on, that would be able to teach them to be good at a variety of skills (including all 12 cognitive processes), and that would make the students employable as well:

- Criminal Justice
- Sports Management
- The Music Business
- The Legal Office
- Military Readiness
- The Fashion Business
- Aerospace Engineering
- Computer Networking
- Homeland Security
- Medical Technology
- Construction
- Computer Programming
- Television Production
- Real Estate Management
- Architecture
- The Banking Industry
- Automotive Engineering
- Architecture
- Biotechnology
- Film Making
- Travel Planning
- Financial Management
- Parenting and Childcare
- Starting an Online Business
- Urban Planning
- Hotel Management
- Health Sciences
- The Food Industry
- Graphic Arts
- Communication
- Veterinary Science
- Marketing
- Telecommunications
- Scientific Reasoning

Obviously, this list could be much longer. The intention here is to make any student excited about learning because what he or she wants to learn about is offered. The trick for the designers of the curricula is to make sure that students' interest is grabbed and maintained for a full year, while teaching them how to hone their capabilities at the 12 cognitive processes.

What are the obstacles?

What would prevent this from happening? Really there are only four issues:

Finding people who know how to build the curricula
Paying the people who will build the curricula
Convincing schools or other entities to offer the curricula
Training teachers to be mentors in these curricula

Smart, articulate, people who are well organized and can write well can easily learn to do the bulk of the work involved in building a course as long as they have access to experts and are guided by experienced designers, and the project is run by someone how knows how to run projects. Finding people who can do this work is not a problem. Being able to pay them for the year or so that it takes to do the work is the real issue.

This leads us to discuss who would pay for this. The answer should be the federal government, but it is clear that that will never happen. The federal government, as any interested citizen knows, is influenced mightily by big business, especially when big business has profits to protect.

Companies that produce textbooks and companies that produce and grade exams will not stand by and see their revenues drop. Any alternative curriculum that did not use textbooks and did not use standardized tests would be anathema to them. Companies that have billions of dollars in revenues from textbooks know how to encourage politicians to protect their interests.

What about the testing industry? A recent report says that "the testing industry is somewhat secretive." I wonder why. But sometimes they do report revenue. To give an example, the revenue of Kaplan Inc., which is just one of many test preparation companies, was over $1 billion in 2008. Who owns Kaplan? *The Washington Post.* So while the testing companies make great profits, the nation's newspapers, having a vested interest in those profits, tout testing as the country's salvation. The most visible touter is the Secretary of Education, who gives eloquent speeches about more rigorous testing that are, of course, printed in *The Washington Post*.

Why would President Obama want to do the same thing as President Bush did, especially when he campaigned against No Child Left Behind, as I pointed out earlier? The answer is simple. There is lots of money invested in testing by powerful players. Kids are no one's main concern.

So the money for the new plan will not be coming from the government.

What about from business? Venture capital, for example?

Is a new kind of high school offered online likely to be a successful business venture? One mentor in the story-centered curriculum can handle between 20 and 50 students, depending on the mentor's experience. Assuming that the students pay tuition that covers the mentor's salary, which means they need to pay at least $3,000 a year, more or less, in tuition, it shouldn't cost anything to run. Charge larger tuitions and there will be profits. Initial investment is about $2 million to build a curriculum, but enough students paying reasonable tuitions will pay that investment back quickly enough. So, is this a big business opportunity?

Actually I doubt it. I think that it is a big opportunity for universities that traditionally charge large tuitions. We have had a great deal of success with master's degrees, for example. But universities typically don't invest $2 million in anything, even if it does have great upside potential. When Carnegie Mellon University made that investment in its West Coast campus (where I was designing the curriculum), it did so without quite knowing it was doing so because the person in charge didn't tell the University officials what he was up to. Universities typically don't think about investing money in order to make money in the daily enterprise. Businesses do think that way, of course, but businesses have trouble starting universities that are accredited. I worked for Trump University, which supposedly was going to do exactly that, but they never could raise enough money or figure out how to be accredited. So there is a potentially very big business in master's degrees, but it needs some well-financed and prescient people to make it happen.

High schools are another story. I actually do not believe that business will invest in online high schools whose mission is to overthrow the existing system. Venture capitalists are not revolutionaries. They tend to follow the herd in whatever they do and there is no herd in education except the one promoting more testing. They certainly do invest in that.

So we are left with appealing to people who actually care about kids and their education. Money isn't and shouldn't be the allure here. This means that the saviors of education will have to be wealthy individuals or foundations started by wealthy individuals.

The health sciences curriculum that we built was funded by the Ewing Kauffman Foundation. We built it using our not-for-profit company, Engines for Education. I really believe that no alternative to the nonprofit model funded by wealthy people exists. We just have to find people who care about education. They are in short supply, and they typically aren't the wealthy people who make pronouncements about education, but I am hopeful that they are out there.

I wouldn't mind being wrong about anything I have said here. The federal government could get taken over by people who actually care about kids and not votes.

How do we convince schools to offer these curricula once they have been developed? It won't be easy. There aren't that many schools run by people who realize that the system is broken. But they do exist, however. The real problem is not so much convincing the head of a private school or the superintendent of a school district. It is more about convincing parents who fundamentally do not understand education, or teachers who have taught what they have always taught and really don't want to learn new skills.

And, in addition, there are all those state standards. The first thing that any school that wants to use our curriculum has to do is to see how they can map what we will teach into their state's standards. If the state standards specify 2 years of algebra, we are out of luck. If they have vague science standards, we are in better shape. Either way, the state standards, passed by all those brilliant state legislatures that know all there is to know about what should be taught in high school, inhibit real change in the system.

So we need motivated heads of schools or school systems, in states that have flexible standards, where parents who hold views about why school was better in their day do not have to be listened to. Do these exist?

Sure.

The last issue is training teachers to mentor. We do this by having teachers be students in a curriculum mentored by others who have experience in that curriculum. Mentoring does not come naturally to people who have been teaching in the usual way. But they pick it up and often find that they like it better.

Here is Lynn Carter, one of the first mentors we trained to teach in this new way at CMU's West Coast campus. He is a professor of software engineering at Carnegie Mellon University.

> It has taken me a while to figure out how to undo about 25 years of teaching experience that was standing in front of a room and talking, but I really like it. I enjoy interacting with students. As much as I enjoy standing in front of students and talking, it is much more satisfying to be dealing with smaller groups, more of a one-on-one interaction.
>
> Professors often complain that no students come to see them during their office hours. That isn't a problem with us here.

How did we teach Professor Carter to mentor Socratically? It wasn't trivial to do, but it didn't take that long either. Once a teacher gets the idea that his job is not telling but helping, he gets into the swing of it fairly easily. Training teachers to teach in the kinds of SCCs we propose for high school is more an issue of familiarizing them with the content, which will differ considerably from what they have been teaching. Handholding comes naturally to most people because they have been doing that kind of teaching all their lives with siblings and children. Lecturing is not a natural human activity and teachers are easily dissuaded from doing it as long as they are not being presented with a classroom of listeners.

In the end, the real question is this: Why do we still have schools?

This is a little like asking why we still have religious institutions. In fact, it is a lot like asking that question because you will get the same reactions. People get used to the institutions that have always been a part of their lives. The fact is that these institutions were created in a different time when knowledge was harder to come by and the economy was quite different.

Religion is not my issue. Should we still have schools?

Instead of answering this question by listing all the good things that schools provide—no one would argue that a literate population is a bad thing, for example—I will turn the question around: What is bad about having schools?

Here is a list of what is bad. Following the list, I will explain what is bad about these things (assuming it isn't obvious).

Schools emphasize competition.
Schools make kids stressed.
Schools know the right answers.
Schools enable bullying and peer pressure.
Schools stifle curiosity.
Schools choose the subjects for students.
Schools have classrooms.
Schools give grades.
Schools provide certification.
Schools confine children.
Schools claim that academics are the winners.
Schools do not value practical skills.
Schools cause students to want to please teachers.
Schools cause students to question their self-worth.
Schools are run by politicians.
Governments use education for repression.
Discovery is not valued in school.
Boredom is seen as a bad thing in school.

Competition: Why should school be a competitive event? Why do we ask how a kid is doing in school? Learning in life outside of school is not a competitive event. We learn what we choose to know in real life.

Stress: When 6-year-olds are stressed about going to school, you know that something is wrong. Is learning in real life stressful? Stress can't be helping kids learn. What kid wouldn't happily skip school on any given day? What does this tell us about the experience?

Right answers: School teaches that there are right answers. The teacher knows them. The test makers know them. Now you have to know them. But in real life, there are very few right answers. Life isn't mathematics. Thinking about how to behave in a situation, planning your day or your life, plotting a strategy for your company or your country—no right answers.

Bullying and peer pressure: You wouldn't have to have *say no to drugs or cigarettes* campaigns if kids didn't go to school. In school there are always other kids telling you how to dress, how to act, how to be cool. Why do we want kids' peer groups to be the true teachers of children? Being left out terrorizes children. Why do we allow this to happen by creating places that foster this behavior?

Stifling of curiosity: Isn't it obvious that learning is really about curiosity? Adults learn about things they want to learn about. Before the age of 6, prior to school, one kid becomes a dinosaur specialist, while another knows all about dog breeds. Outside of school, people drive their own learning. Schools eliminate this natural behavior.

Subjects chosen for you: Why algebra, physics, economics, and U.S. history? Because those subjects were pretty exciting to the president of Harvard in 1892. And, if you are interested in something else—psychology, business, medicine, computers, design? Too bad. Those subjects weren't taught at Harvard in 1892. Is that nuts or what?

Classrooms: If you wanted to learn something and had the money, wouldn't you hire someone to be your mentor, and have them be there for you while you tried out learning the new thing? Isn't that what small children have, a parent ready to teach as needed. Classrooms make no sense as a venue for learning unless, of course, you want to save money and have 30 (or, worse, hundreds of) students handled by one teacher. Once you have ratios like that, you have to teach by talking and then hoping someone was listening, so then you have to have tests. Schools cannot work as places of learning if they employ classrooms. And, of course, they pretty much all do.

Grades: Any professor can tell you that students are pretty much concerned with whether what you are telling them will be on the test and what they might do for extra credit. In other words, they want a good grade. If you tell them that $2 + 2 = 5$ and it will be on the test, they will tell you that $2 + 2 = 5$ if it means getting a good grade. Parents do not give grades to children and employers do not give grades to employees. They judge their work and progress for sure, but not by assigning numbers to a report card.

Certification: We all know why people attend college. They do so primarily to say they are college graduates so they can get a job or go on to a professional school. Most don't care all that much about what hoops they have to go through. They do what they are told. Similarly, students try to get through high school so they can go on to college. As long as students are not in school to get an education, you can be pretty sure they won't get one. Most of our graduates have learned to jump through hoops, nothing more.

Confined children: Children like to run around. Is this news to anyone? They have a difficult time sitting still and they learn by trying things out and asking questions. Of course, in school sitting still is the norm. So we have come up with this wonderful idea of ADHD, that is, drug those who won't sit still into submission. Is the system sick or what?

Academics viewed as winners: Who are the smartest kids in school? The ones who are good at math and science, of course. Why do we think that? Who knows? We just do. Those who are good at these subjects go on to be professors. So those are certainly the smartest people we have in our society. Perhaps they are. But I can tell you from personal experience that our society doesn't respect professors all that much, so something is wrong here.

Practical skills not valued: When I was young, there were academic high schools and trade high schools. Trade high schools were for dumb kids. Academic high schools were for smart kids. We all thought this made sense. Except that are a lot of unemployed English majors and a lot of employed airplane mechanics. Where did we get the idea that education was about scholarship? This is not what Ben Franklin thought when our system was being designed, but he was outvoted.

The need to please teachers: People who succeed at school are invariably people who are good at figuring out what the teacher wants and giving it to her. In real life there is no teacher to please and these "grade grubbers" often find themselves lost. When I did graduate admissions, if a student presented an undergraduate record with all A's, I immediately rejected him. There was no way he was equally good at or equally interested in everything (except pleasing the teacher). As a professor, I had no patience for students who thought that telling me what I just told them was the essence of academic achievement.

Self-worth questioned: School is full of winners and losers. I graduated number 322 in my high school class (out of 678). Notice that I remember this. Do you think this was good for my self-esteem? Even the guy who graduated number 2 felt like a loser. In school, most everyone sees themselves as a loser. Why do we allow this to happen?

Politicians in charge: Politicians demand reform but they wouldn't know reform if it hit them over the head. What they mean is that school should be like they remember rather than how it is now, and they will work hard to get you to vote for them to give them money to restore the system to the awful state it always was in. Politicians, no matter what party, actually have no interest in education at all. An educated electorate makes campaigning much harder.

Government use of education for repression: As long as there have been governments, there have been governments that wanted people to think that the government (and the country) is very good. We all recognize this tendency in dictatorships that promote the marvels of the dictator and rewrite history whenever it is convenient. When you point out that our government does the same thing, you are roundly booed. We all know that the Indians were savages that Abraham Lincoln was a great president and that we are the freest country on earth. School is about teaching "truth."

Discovery not valued: The most important things we learn we teach ourselves. This is why kids have trouble learning from their parents' experience. They need their own experiences to ponder and to learn from. We need to try things out and see how they go. This kind of learning is not valued in school because it might lead to, heaven forbid, failure, and failure is a really bad word in school. Except failure is how we learn, which is pretty much why school doesn't work.

Boredom ignored: Boredom is a bad thing. We drug bored kids with Ritalin so they will stop being bored. All of my best work has come when I was most bored and let my mind wander. It is odd that we keep trying to prevent this from happening with kids. Lots of TV, that's the ticket.

Major learning-by-doing mechanism ignored: And last but not least, scholars from Plato to Dewey have pointed that people learn by doing. That is how we learn. Doing. Got it? Apparently not. Very little doing in schools. Unless you count filling in circles with number 2 pencils as doing.

Online education can change all this. Build it right once and children the world over will have the opportunity to learn how to think and to learn how to work. Such a system would be capable of changing fast. Any new industry or market or technology could produce a course in what is needed to work in that field and instantly get the people it needed.

Schools are an ancient artifact that can't last much longer.

Notes

Chapter 1

1. In the United States it all stems from a meeting of the Committee of Ten chaired by the president of Harvard in 1892.

2. John Adams, the second president of the United States, said that school should teach us how to live and teach us how to make a living. No subsequent U.S. president has ever understood this point, however.

Chapter 2

1. Paul Ramsden. *Learning to Teach in Higher Education*. New York: Routledge, 1992.

2. Arthur W. Chickering and Zelda F. Gamson. "Seven Principles for Good Practice in Undergraduate Education." *The American Association for Higher Education Bulletin*, March 1987.

3. John V. Adams, Student Evaluations: The Ratings Game. *Inquiry*, 1(2), Fall 1997, 10–16.

Chapter 3

1. From a column by Robert Jamieson, Jr., Seattle PI.com, February 27, 2008.

2. I didn't start writing about education until 1978. Before that it was always artificial intelligence that concerned me.

3. I have done this in gory detail in *Dynamic Memory* and in *Dynamic Memory Revisited* as well as in *Explanation Patterns*.

4. *Tell Me a Story*.

Chapter 5

1. For more on the origins of the school system, see *The Origins of the American High School* as well as *Making Minds Less Well Educated Than Our Own*.

2. Socratic Arts, a company that builds learning-by-doing software for schools, businesses, and government.

Chapter 7

1. Report Urges Changes in Teaching Math, *New York Times*, March 14, 2008.

2. Daniel Willingham, *Why Don't Students Like School: A Cognitive Scientist Answers Questions About How the Mind Works and What It Means for the Classroom*. San Francisco: Jossey Bass, 2010.

Chapter 8

1. *Scripts, Plans, Goals and Understanding* (1977) and *Dynamic Memory* (1981).

Chapter 9

1. I wrote about this in some detail in *The Future of Decision Making* and have been building this kind of thing for big corporations.

2. There are many experiences one could build. I talked about some that we have built for high school and graduate school in Chapter 8. At the end of this chapter, I talk about one for little kids.

3. *Scripts, Plans, Goals, and Understanding*.

4. For example, *Dynamic Memory* and *Inside CBR*.

5. Richard Neustadt and Ernest May, *Thinking in Time: The Uses of History For Decision Makers*, Washington, D.C.: Free Press, 1988.

6. Taken from *Smart Parenting*, Brad Smart and Kate Smart. Mursau: CDK Press, 2007.

7. Roger Fisher, author of *Getting to Yes*.

8. Blaise Pascal usually gets the credit.

About the Author

Roger Schank is the CEO of Socratic Arts and Managing Director of Engines for Education. He was Chief Education Officer of Carnegie Mellon West, Distinguished Career Professor in the School of Computer Science at Carnegie Mellon University, and Chief Learning Officer of Trump University. He founded the renowned Institute for the Learning Sciences at Northwestern University, where he is John P. Evans Professor Emeritus in Computer Science, Education, and Psychology. He has taught at Yale University, the University of Paris VII, and Stanford University. He holds a Ph.D. in linguistics from the University of Texas. He is a fellow of the AAAI and was founder of the Cognitive Science Society and co-founder of the *Journal of Cognitive Science*. He is the author of more than 25 books on learning, language, artificial intelligence, education, memory, reading, e-learning, and storytelling. Recently he has been consulting with businesses about how to be more innovative, and how to manage their corporate knowledge so that it is delivered just in time.